The making of a bigot

by

Rose Macaulay

ISBN: 978-1-63923-217-8

Printed: May 2022

Cover Art By: Amit Paul

Published and Distributed By:
Lushena Books
607 Country Club Drive, Unit E
Bensenville, IL 60106
www.lushenabooksinc.com/books

ISBN: 978-1-63923-217-8

THE MAKING OF A BIGOT

BY
ROSE MACAULAY
Author of "The Lee Shore," "Views and Vagabonds," etc.

HODDER AND STOUGHTON
LONDON   NEW YORK   TORONTO

TO D. F. C.

"How various is man! How multiplied his experience, his outlook, his conclusions!"—H. Belloc.

"And every single one of them is right."—R. Kipling.

"The rational human faith must armour itself with prejudice in an age of prejudices."—G. K. Chesterton.

CONTENTS

CHAPTER I.

CAMBRIDGE.

IT was Trinity Sunday, full of buttercups and cuckoos and the sun. In Cambridge it was a Scarlet Day. In colleges, people struggling through a desert of Tripos papers or Mays rested their souls for a brief space in a green oasis, and took their lunch up the river. In Sunday schools, teachers were telling of the shamrock, that ill-considered and peculiarly inappropriate image conceived by a hard-pressed saint. Everywhere people were being ordained.

Miss Jamison met Eddy Oliver in Petty Cury, while she was doing some house-to-house visiting with a bundle of leaflets that looked like tracts. She looked at him vaguely, then suddenly began to take an interest in him.

"Of course," she said, with decision, "you've got to join, too."

"Rather," he said. "Tell me what it is. I'm sure it's full of truth."

"It's the National Service League. I'm a working associate, and I'm persuading people to join. It's a good thing, really. Were you at the meeting yesterday?"

"No, I missed that. I was at another meeting, in point of fact. I often am, you know." He said it with a touch of mild perplexity. It was so true.

She was turning over the sheaf of tracts.

"Let me see: which will meet your case? Leaflet M, the Modern Sisyphus—that's a picture one, and more for the poor; so simple and graphic. P is better for you. Have you ever thought what war is, and what it would be like to have it raging round your own home? Have you ever thought what your feelings would be if you heard that an enemy had landed on these shores, and you knew that you were ignorant of the means by which you could help to defend your country and your home? You probably think that if you are a member of a rifle club, and know how to shoot, you have done all that is needed. But—well, you haven't, and so on, you know. You'd better take P. And Q. Q says 'Are you a Liberal? Then join the League, because, etc. Are you a Democrat? Are you a Socialist? Are you a Conservative? Are you——' "

"Yes," said Eddy, "I'm everything of that sort. It won't be able to think of anything I'm not."

She thought he was being funny, though he wasn't; he was speaking the simple truth.

"Anyhow," she said, "you'll find good reasons there why you should join, whatever you are. Just think, you know, suppose the Germans landed." She supposed that for a little, then got on to physical training and military discipline, how important they are.

Eddy said when she paused, "Quite. I think you are utterly right." He always did, when anyone explained anything to him; he was like that; he had a receptive mind.

"You can become," said Miss Jamison, getting to the gist of the matter, "a guinea member, or a penny adherent, or a shilling associate, or a more classy sort of associate, that pays five shillings and gets all kinds of literature."

"I'll be that," said Eddy Oliver, who liked nearly all kinds of literature.

So Miss Jamison got out her book of vouchers on the spot, and enrolled him, receiving five shillings and presenting a blue button on which was inscribed the remark, "The Path of Duty is the Path of Safety."

"So true," said Eddy. "A jolly good motto. A jolly good League. I'll tell everyone I meet to join."

"There'll be another meeting," said Miss Jamison, "next Thursday. Of course you'll come. We want a good audience this time, if possible. We never have one, you know. There'll be lantern slides, illustrating invasion as it would be now, and invasion as it would be were the National Service League Bill passed. Tremendously exciting."

Eddy made a note of it in his Cambridge Pocket Diary, a small and profusely inscribed volume without which he never moved, as his engagements were numerous, and his head not strong.

He wrote below June 8th, "N.S.L., 8 p.m., Guildhall, small room." For the same date he had previously inscribed, "Fabians, 7.15, Victoria Assembly Rooms," "E.C.U. Protest Meeting, Guildhall, large room, 2.15," and "Primrose League Fête, Great Shelford Manor, 3 p.m." He belonged to all these societies (they are all so utterly right) and many others more esoteric, and led a complex and varied life, full of faith and hope. With so many right points of view in the world, so many admirable, if differing, faiths, whither, he demanded, might not humanity rise? Himself, he joined everything that came his way, from Vegetarian Societies to Heretic Clubs and Ritualist Guilds; all, for him, were full of truth. This attitude of omni-acceptance sometimes puzzled and worried less receptive and more single-minded persons; they were known at times even to accuse him, with tragic injustice, of insincerity. When they did so, he saw how right they were; he entirely sympathised with their point of view.

At this time he was nearly twenty-three, and nearly at the end of his Cambridge career. In person he was a slight youth, with intelligent hazel eyes under sympathetic brows, and easily ruffled brown hair, and a general air of receptive impressionability. Clad not unsuitably in grey flannels and the soft hat of the year (soft hats vary importantly from age to age), he strolled down King's Parade. There he met a man of his own college; this was liable to occur in King's Parade. The man said he was going to tea with his people, and Eddy was to come too. Eddy did so. He liked the Denisons; they were full of generous enthusiasm for certain things—(not, like Eddy himself, for everything). They wanted Votes for Women, and Liberty for Distressed Russians, and spinning-looms for everyone. They had inspired Eddy to want these things, too; he belonged, indeed, to societies for promoting each of them. On the other hand, they did not want Tariff Reform, or Conscription, or Prayer Book Revision (for they seldom read the Prayer Book), and if they had known that Eddy belonged also to societies for promoting these objects, they would have remonstrated with him.

Professor Denison was a quiet person, who said little, but listened to his wife and children. He had much sense of humour, and some imagination. He was fifty-five. Mrs. Denison was a small and engaging lady, a tremendous worker in good causes; she had little sense of humour, and a vivid, if often misapplied, imagination. She was forty-six. Her son Arnold was tall, lean, cynical, intelligent, edited a university magazine (the most interesting of them), was president of a Conversation Society, and was just going into his uncle's publishing house. He had plenty of sense of humour (if he had had less, he would have bored himself to death), and an imagination kept within due bounds. He was twenty-three. His sister Margery was also intelligent, but, notwithstanding this, had recently published a book of verse; some of it was not so bad as a great many people's verse. She also designed wall-papers, which on the whole she did better. She had an unequal sense of humour, keen in certain directions, blunt in others, like most people's; the same description applies to her imagination. She was twenty-two.

Eddy and Arnold found them having tea in the garden, with two brown undergraduates and a white one. The Denisons belonged to the East and West Society, which tries to effect a union between the natives of these two quarters of the globe. It has conversazioni, at which the brown men congregate at one end of the room and the white men at the other, and both, one hopes, are happy. This afternoon Mrs. Denison and her daughter were each talking to a brown young man (Downing and Christ's), and the white young man (Trinity Hall) was being silent with Professor Denison, because East is East and West is West, and never the twain shall meet, and really, you can't talk to blacks. Arnold joined the West; Eddy, who belonged to the above-mentioned society, helped Miss Denison to talk to her black.

Rather soon the East went, and the West became happier.

Miss Denison said, "Dorothy Jamison came round this afternoon, wanting us to join the National Service League or something."

Mrs. Denison said, snippily, "Dorothy ought to know better," at the same moment that Eddy said, "It's a jolly little League, apparently. Quite full of truth."

The Hall man said that his governor was a secretary or something at home, and kept having people down to speak at meetings. So he and the Denisons argued about it, till Margery said, "Oh, well, of course, you're hopeless. But I don't know what Eddy means by it. *You* don't want to encourage militarism, surely, Eddy."

Eddy said surely yes, shouldn't one encourage everything? But really, and no ragging, Margery persisted, he didn't belong to a thing like that?

Eddy showed his blue button.

"Rather, I do. Have you ever thought what war is, and what it would be like to have it raging round your own home? Are you a democrat? Then join the League."

"Idiot," said Margery, who knew him well enough to call him so.

"He believes in everything. I believe in nothing," Arnold explained. "He accepts; I refuse. He likes three lumps of sugar in his tea; I like none. He had better be a journalist, and write for the *Daily Mail*, the *Clarion*, and the *Spectator*."

"What *are* you going to do when you go down?" Margery asked Eddy, suspiciously.

Eddy blushed, because he was going for a time to work in a Church settlement. A man he knew was a clergyman there, and had convinced him that it was his duty and he must. The Denisons did not care about Church settlements, only secular ones; that, and because he had a clear, pale skin that showed everything, was why he blushed.

"I'm going to work with some men in Southwark," he said, embarrassed. "Anyhow, for a time. Help with boys' clubs, you know, and so on."

"Parsons?" inquired Arnold, and Eddy admitted it, where upon Arnold changed the subject; he had no concern with Parsons.

The Denisons were so shocked at Eddy, that they let the Hall man talk about the South African match for quite two minutes.

They were probably afraid that if they didn't Eddy might talk about the C.I.C.C.U., which would be infinitely worse. Eddy was perhaps the only man at the moment in Cambridge who belonged simultaneously to the C.I.C.C.U., the Church Society, and the Heretics. (It may be explained for the benefit of the uninitiated that the C.I.C.C.U. is Low Church, and the Church Society is High Church, and the Heretics is no church at all. They are all admirable societies).

Arnold said presently, interrupting the match, "If I keep a second-hand bookshop in Soho, will you help me, Eddy?"

Eddy said he would like to.

"It will be awfully good training for both of us," said Arnold. "You'll see much more life that way, you know, than at your job in Southwark."

Arnold had manfully overcome his distaste for alluding to Eddy's job in Southwark, in order to make a last attempt to snatch a brand from the burning.

But Eddy, thinking he might as well be hanged for a sheep as a lamb, said,

"You see, my people rather want me to take Orders, and the Southwark job is by way of finding out if I want to or not. I'm nearly sure I don't, you know," he added, apologetically, because the Denisons were looking so badly disappointed in him.

Mrs. Denison said kindly, "I think I should tell your people straight out that you can't. It's a tiresome little jar, I know, but honestly, I don't believe it's a bit of use members of a family pretending that they see life from the same angle when they don't."

Eddy said, "Oh, but I think we do, in a way. Only——"

It was really rather difficult to explain. He did indeed see life from the same angle as the rest of his family, but from many other angles as well, which was confusing. The question was, could one select some one thing to be, clergyman or anything else, unless one was very sure that it implied no negations, no exclusions of the other angles? That was, perhaps, what his life in Southwark would teach him. Most of the clergy round his own home—and, his father being a Dean, he knew many—hadn't, it seemed to him, learnt the art of acceptance; they kept drawing lines, making sheep and goat divisions, like the Denisons.

The Hall man, feeling a little embarrassed because they were getting rather intimate and personal, and probably would like to get more so if he were not there, went away. He had had to call on the Denisons, but they weren't his sort, he knew. Miss Denison and her parents frightened him, and he didn't get on with girls who dressed artistically, or wrote poetry, and Arnold Denison was a conceited crank, of course. Oliver was a good sort, only very thick with Denison for some reason. If he was Oliver, and wanted to do anything so dull as slumming with parsons in Southwark, he wouldn't be put off by anything the Denisons said.

"Why don't *you* get your tie to match your socks, Eddy?" Arnold asked, with a yawn, when Egerton had gone.

His mother, a hospitable lady, and kind to Egertons and all others who came to her house, told him not to be disagreeable. Eddy said, truly, that he wished he did, and that it was a capital idea and looked charming.

"Egertons do look rather charming, quite often," Margery conceded. "I suppose that's something after all."

Mrs. Denison added, (exquisite herself, she had a taste for neatness): "Their hair and their clothes are always beautifully brushed; which is more than yours are, Arnold."

Arnold lay back with his eyes shut, and groaned gently. Egerton had fatigued him very much.

Eddy thought it was rather nice of Mrs. Denison and Margery to be kind about Egerton because he had been to tea. He realised that he himself was the only person there who was neither kind nor unkind about Egerton, because he really liked him. This the Denisons would have hopelessly failed to understand, or, probably, to believe; if he had mentioned it they would have thought he was being kind, too. Eddy liked a number of people who were ranked by the Denisons among the goats; even the rowing men of his own college, which happened to be a college where one didn't row.

Mrs. Denison asked Eddy if he would come to lunch on Thursday to meet some of the Irish players, whom they were putting up for the week. The Denisons, being intensely English and strong Home Rulers, felt, besides the artistic admiration for the Abbey Theatre players common to all, a political enthusiasm for them as Nationalists, so putting three of them up was a delightful hospitality. Eddy, who shared both the artistic and the political enthusiasm, was delighted to come to lunch. Unfortunately he would have to hurry away afterwards to the Primrose League Fête at Great Shelford, but he did not mention this.

Consulting his watch, he found he was even now due at a meeting of a Sunday Games Club to which he belonged, so he said goodbye to the Denisons and went.

"Mad as a hatter," was Arnold's languid comment on him when he had gone; "but well-intentioned."

"But," said Margery, "I can't gather that he intends anything at all. He's so absurdly indiscriminate."

"He intends everything," her father interpreted. "You all, in this intense generation, intend much too much; Oliver carries it a little further than most of you, that's all. His road to his ultimate destination is most remarkably well-paved."

"Oh, poor boy," said Mrs. Denison, remonstrating. She went in to finish making arrangements for a Suffrage meeting.

Margery went to her studio to hammer jewellery for the Arts and Crafts Exhibition.

Professor Denison went to his study to look over Tripos papers.

Arnold lay in the garden and smoked. He was the least energetic of his family, and not industrious.

CHAPTER II.

ST. GREGORY'S.

PROBABLY, Eddy decided, after working for a week in Southwark, the thing to be was a clergyman. Clergymen get their teeth into something; they make things move; you can see results, which is so satisfactory. They can point to a man, or a society, and say, "Here you are; I made this. I found him a worm and no man, and left him a human being," or, "I found them scattered and unmoral units, and left them a Band of Hope, or a Mothers' Union." It is a great work. Eddy caught the spirit of it, and threw himself vigorously into men's clubs and lads' brigades, and boy scouts, and all the other organisations that flourished in the parish of St. Gregory, under the Reverend Anthony Finch and his assistant clergy. Father Finch, as he was called in the parish, was a stout, bright man, shrewd, and merry, and genial, and full of an immense energy and power of animating the inanimate. He had set all kinds of people and institutions on their feet, and given them a push to start them and keep them in motion. So his parish was a live parish, in a state of healthy circulation. Father Finch was emphatically a worker. Dogma and ritual, though certainly essential to his view of life, did not occupy the prominent place given to them by, for instance, his senior curate, Hillier. Hillier was the supreme authority on ecclesiastical ceremonial. It was he who knew, without referring to a book, all the colours of all the festivals and vigils; and what cere-cloths and maniples were; it was he who decided how many candles were demanded at the festal evensong of each saint, and what vestments were suitable to be worn in procession, and all the other things that lay people are apt to think get done for themselves, but which really give a great deal of trouble and thought to some painstaking organiser.

Hillier had genial and sympathetic manners with the poor, was very popular in the parish, belonged to eight religious guilds, wore the badges of all of them on his watch-chain, and had been educated at a county school and a theological college. The junior curate, James Peters, was a jolly young cricketer of twenty-four, and had been at Marlborough and Cambridge with Eddy, he was, in fact, the man who had persuaded Eddy to come and help in St. Gregory's.

There were several young laymen working in the parish. St. Gregory's House, which was something between a clergy house and a settlement, spread wide nets to catch workers. Hither drifted bank clerks in their leisure hours, eager to help with clubs in the evenings and Sunday school classes on Sundays. Here also came undergraduates in the vacations, keen to plunge into the mêlée, and try their hands at social and philanthropic enterprises; some of them were going to take Orders later, some were not; some were stifling with ardent work troublesome doubts as to the object of the universe, others were not; all were full of the generous idealism of the first twenties. When Eddy went there, there were no undergraduates, but several visiting lay workers.

Between the senior and junior curates came the second curate, Bob Traherne, an ardent person who belonged to the Church Socialist League. Eddy joined this League at once. It is an interesting one to belong to, and has an exciting, though some think old-fashioned, programme. Seeing him inclined to join things, Hillier set before him, diplomatically, the merits of the various Leagues and Guilds and Fraternities whose badges he wore, and for which new recruits are so important.

"Anyone who cares for the principles of the Church," he said, shyly eager, having asked Eddy into his room to smoke one Sunday evening after supper, "must support the objects of the G.S.C." He explained what they were, and why. "You see, worship can't be complete without it—not so much because it's a beautiful thing in itself, and certainly not from the æsthetic or sensuous point of view, though of course there's that appeal too, and particularly to the poor—but because it's used in the other branches, and we must join up and come into line as far as we conscientiously can."

"Quite," said Eddy, seeing it. "Of course we must."

"You'll join the Guild, then?" said Hillier, and Eddy said, "Oh, yes, I'll join," and did so. So Hillier had great hopes for him, and told him about the F.I.S., and the L.M.G.

But Traherne said afterwards to Eddy, "Don't you go joining Hillier's little Fraternities and Incense Guilds. They won't do you any good. Leave them to people like Robinson and Wilkes." (Robinson and Wilkes were two young clerks who came to work in the parish and adored Hillier.) "They seem to find such things necessary to their souls; in fact, they tell me they are starved without them; so I suppose they must be allowed to have them. But you simply haven't the time to spend."

"Oh, I think it's right, you know," said Eddy, who never rejected anything or fell in with negations. That was where he drew his line—he went along with all points of view so long as they were positive: as soon as condemnation or rejection came in, he broke off.

Traherne puffed at his pipe rather scornfully.

"It's not right," he grunted, "and it's not wrong. It's neuter. Oh, have it as you like. It's all very attractive, of course; I'm entirely in sympathy with the objects of all these guilds, as you know. It's only the guilds themselves I object to—a lot of able-bodied people wasting their forces banding themselves together to bring about relatively trivial and unimportant things, when there's all the work of the shop waiting to be done. Oh, I don't mean Hillier doesn't work—of course he's first-class—but the more of his mind he gives to incense and stoles, the less he'll have to give to the work that matters—and it's not as if he had such an immense deal of it altogether—mind, I mean."

"But after all," Eddy demurred, "if that sort of thing appeals to anybody...."

"Oh, let 'em have it, let 'em have it," said Traherne wearily. "Let 'em all have what they like; but don't *you* be dragged into a net of millinery and fuss. Even you will surely admit that things don't all matter equally—that it's more important, for instance, that people should learn a little about profit-sharing than a great deal about church ornaments; more important that they should use leadless glaze than that they should use incense. Well, then, there you are; go for the essentials, and let the incidentals look after themselves."

"Oh, let's go for everything," said Eddy with enthusiasm. "It's all worth having."

The second curate regarded him with a cynical smile, and gave him up as a bad job. But anyhow, he had joined the Church Socialist League, whose members according to themselves, do go for the essentials, and, according to some other people, go to the devil; anyhow go, or endeavour to go, somewhere, and have no superfluous energy to spend on toys by the roadside. Only Eddy Oliver seemed to have energy to spare for every game that turned up. He made himself rather useful, and taught the boys' clubs single-stick and boxing, and played billiards and football with them.

The only thing that young James Peters wanted him to join was a Rugby football club. Teach the men and boys of the parish to play Rugger like sportsmen and not like cads, and you've taught them most of what a boy or man need learn, James Peters held. While the senior curate said, give them the ritual of the Catholic Church, and the second curate said, give them a minimum wage, and the vicar said, put into them, by some means or another, the fear of God, the junior curate led them to the playing-field hired at great expense, and tried to make sportsmen of them; and grew at times, but very seldom, passionate like a thwarted child, because it was the most difficult thing he had ever tried to do, and because they would lose their tempers and kick one another on the shins, and walk off the field, and send in their resignations, together with an intimation that St. Gregory's Church would see them no more, because the referee was a liar and didn't come it fair. Then James Peters would throw back their resignations and their intimations in their faces, and call them silly asses and generally manage to smooth things down in his cheerful, youthful, vigorous way. Eddy Oliver helped him in this. He and Peters were great friends, though more unlike even than most people are. Peters had a very single eye, and herded people very easily and completely into sheep and goats; his particular nomenclature for them was "sportsmen" and "rotters." He took the Catholic Church, so to speak, in his swing, and was one of her most loyal and energetic sons.

To him, Arnold Denison, whom he had known slightly at Cambridge, was decidedly a goat. Arnold Denison came, at

Eddy's invitation, to supper at St. Gregory's House one Sunday night. The visit was not a success. Hillier, usually the life of any party he adorned, was silent, and on his guard. Arnold, at times a tremendous talker, said hardly a word through the meal. Eddy knew of old that he was capable, in uncongenial society, of an unmannerly silence, which looked scornful partly because it was scornful, and partly because of Arnold's rather cynical physiognomy, which sometimes unjustly suggested mockery. On this Sunday evening he was really less scornful than simply aloof; he had no concern with these people, nor they with him; they made each other mutually uncomfortable. Neither could have anything to say to the other's point of view. Eddy, the connecting link, felt unhappy about it. What was the matter with the idiots, that they wouldn't understand each other? It seemed to him extraordinarily stupid. But undoubtedly the social fault lay with Arnold, who was being rude. The others, as hosts, tried to make themselves pleasant—even Hillier, who quite definitely didn't like Arnold, and who was one of those who as a rule think it right and true to their colours to show disapproval when they feel it. The others weren't like that (the difference perhaps was partly between the schools which had respectively reared them), so they were agreeable with less effort.

But the meal was not a success. It began with grace, which, in spite of its rapidity and its decent cloak of Latin, quite obviously shocked and embarrassed Arnold. ("Stupid of him," thought Eddy; "he might have known we'd say it here.") It went on with Peters talking about his Rugger club, which bored Arnold. This being apparent, the Vicar talked about some Cambridge men they both knew. As the men had worked for a time in St. Gregory's parish, Arnold had already given them up as bad jobs, so hadn't much to say about them, except one, who had turned over a new leaf, and now helped to edit a new weekly paper. Arnold mentioned this paper with approbation.

"Did you see last week's?" he asked the Vicar. "There were some extraordinarily nice things in it."

As no one but Eddy had seen last week's, and everyone but Eddy thought *The Heretic* in thoroughly bad taste, if not worse, the subject was not a general success. Eddy referred to a play that had been reviewed in it. That seemed a good subject; plays are a friendly, uncontroversial topic. But between Arnold and clergymen no topic seemed friendly. Hillier introduced a popular play of the hour which had a religious trend. He even asked Arnold if he had seen it. Arnold said no, he had missed that pleasure. Hillier said it was grand, simply grand; he had been three times.

"Of course," he added, "one's on risky ground, and one isn't quite sure how far one likes to see such marvellous religious experiences represented on the stage. But the spirit is so utterly reverent that one can't feel anything but the rightness of the whole thing. It's a rather glorious triumph of devotional expression."

And that wasn't a happy topic either, for no one but he and Eddy liked the play at all. The Vicar thought it cheap and tawdry; Traherne thought it sentimental and revolting; Peters thought it silly rot; and Arnold had never thought about it at all, but had just supposed it to be absurd, the sort of play to which one would go, if one went at all, to laugh; like "The Sins of Society," or "Everywoman," only rather coarse, too.

Hillier said to Eddy, who had seen the play with him, "Didn't you think it tremendously fine, Oliver?"

Eddy said, "Yes, quite. I really did. But Denison wouldn't like it, you know."

Denison, Hillier supposed, was one of the fools who have said in their hearts, etc. In that case the play in question would probably be an eye-opener for him, and it was a pity he shouldn't see it.

Hillier told him so. "You really ought to see it, Mr. Denison."

Arnold said, "Life, unfortunately, is short."

Hillier, nettled, said, "I'd much rather see 'The Penitent' than all your Shaws put together. I'm afraid I can't pretend to owe any allegiance there."

Arnold, who thought Shaw common, not to say Edwardian, looked unresponsive. Then Traherne began to talk about ground-rents. When Traherne began to talk he as a rule went on. Neither

Hillier nor Arnold, who had mutually shocked one another, said much more. Arnold knew a little about rents, ground and other, and if Traherne had been a layman he would have been interested in talking about them. But he couldn't and wouldn't talk to clergymen; emphatically, he did not like them.

After supper, Eddy took him to his own room to smoke. With his unlit pipe in his hand, Arnold lay back and let out a deep breath of exhaustion.

"You were very rude and disagreeable at supper," said Eddy, striking a match. "It was awkward for me. I must apologise to-morrow for having asked you. I shall say it's your country manners, though I suppose you would like me to say that you don't approve of clergymen.... Really, Arnold, I was surprised you should be so very rustic, even if you don't like them."

Arnold groaned faintly.

"Chuck it," he murmured. "Come out of it before it is too late, before you get sucked in irrevocably. I'll help you; I'll tell the vicar for you; yes, I'll interview them all in turn, even Hillier, if it will make it easier for you. Will it?"

"No," said Eddy. "I'm not going to leave at present. I like being here."

"That," said Arnold, "is largely why it's so demoralising for you. Now for *me* it would be distressing, but innocuous. For you it's poison."

"Well, now," Eddy reasoned with him, "what's the matter with Traherne, for instance? Of course, I see that the vicar's too much the practical man of the world for you, and Peters too much the downright sportsman, and Hillier too much the pious ass (though I like him, you know). But Traherne's clever and all alive, and not in the least reputable. What's the matter with him, then?"

Arnold grunted. "Don't know. Must be something, or he wouldn't be filling his present position in life. Probably he labours under the delusion that life is real, life is earnest. Socialists often do.... Look here, come and see Jane one day, will you? She'd be a change for you."

"What's Jane like?"

"I don't know.... Not like anyone here, anyhow. She draws in pen and ink, and lives in a room in a little court out of Blackfriars Road, with a little fat fair girl called Sally. Sally Peters; she's a cousin of young James here, I believe. Rather like him, too, only rounder and jollier, with bluer eyes and yellower hair. Much more of a person, I imagine; more awake to things in general, and not a bit *rangée*, though quite crude. But the same sort of cheery exuberance; personally, I couldn't live with either; but Jane manages it quite serenely. Sally isn't free of the good-works taint herself, though we hope she is outgrowing it."

"Oh, I've met her. She comes and helps Jimmy with the children's clubs sometimes."

"I expect she does. But, as I say, we're educating her. She's young yet.... Jane is good for her. So are Miss Hogan, and the two Le Moines, and I. We should also be good for *you*, if you could spare us some of your valuable time between two Sunday school classes. Good night. I'm going home now, because it makes me rather sad to be here."

He went home.

The clergy of St. Gregory's thought him (respectively) an ill-mannered and irritating young man, probably clever enough to learn better some day; an infidel, very likely too proud ever to learn better at all, this side the grave; a dilettante slacker, for whom the world hadn't much use; and a conceited crank, for whom James Peters had no use at all. But they didn't like to tell Eddy so.

James Peters, a transparent youth, threw only a thin veil over his opinions, however, when he talked to Eddy about his cousin Sally. He was, apparently, anxious about Sally. Eddy had met her at children's clubs, and thought her a cheery young person, and admired the amber gold of her hair, and her cornflower-blue eyes, and her power of always thinking of a fresh game at the right moment.

"I'm supposed to be keeping an eye upon her," James said. "She has to earn her living, you know, so she binds books and lives in a room off the Blackfriars Road with another girl.... I'm not sure I care about the way they live, to say the truth. They have such queer people in, to supper and so on. Men, you know, of all sorts. I believe Denison goes. They sit on a bed that's meant to look like a sofa and doesn't. And they're only girls—Miss Dawn's older than Sally, but not very old—and they've no one to look after them; it doesn't seem right. And they do know the most extraordinary people. Miss Dawn's rather a queer girl herself, I think; unlike other people, somehow. Very—very detached, if you understand; and doesn't care a rap for the conventions, I should say. That's all very well in its way, and she's a very quiet-mannered person—can't think how she and Sally made friends—but it's a dangerous plan for most people. And some of their friends are ... well, rather rotters, you know. Look like artists, or Fabians, without collars, and so on.... Oh, I forgot—you're a Fabian, aren't you?... Well, anyhow, I should guess that some of them are without morals either; in my experience the two things are jolly apt to go together. There are the Le Moines, now. Have you ever come across either of them?"

"I've just met Cecil Le Moine. He's rather charming, isn't he?"

"The sort of person," said James Peters, "for whom I have no use whatever. No, he doesn't appear to me charming. An effeminate ass, I call him. Oh, I know he calls himself frightfully clever and all that, and I suppose he thinks he's good-looking ... but as selfish as sin. Anyhow, he and his wife couldn't live together, so they parted before their first year was over. Her music worried him or something, and prevented him concentrating his precious brain on his literary efforts; and I suppose he got on her nerves, too. I believe they agreed quite pleasantly to separate, and are quite pleased to meet each other about the place, and are rather good friends. But I call it pretty beastly, looking at marriage like that. If they'd hated each other there'd have been more excuse. And she's a great friend of Miss Dawn's, and Sally's developed what I consider an inordinate affection for her; and she and Miss Dawn between them have simply got hold of her—Sally, I mean—and are upsetting her and giving her all kinds of silly new points of view. She doesn't come half as often to the clubs as she used. And she was tremendously keen on the Church, and—and really religious, you know—and she's getting quite different. I feel sort of responsible, and it's worrying me rather."

He puffed discontentedly at his pipe.

"Pity to get less keen on anything," Eddy mused. "New points of view seem to me all to the good; it's losing hold of the old that's a mistake. Why let anything go, ever?"

"She's getting to think it doesn't matter," James complained; "Church, and all that. I know she's given up things she used to do. And really, the more she's surrounded by influences such as Mrs. Le Moine's, the more she needs the Church to pull her through, if only she'd see it. Mrs. Le Moine's a wonderful musician, I suppose, but she has queer ideas, rather; I shouldn't trust her. She and Hugh Datcherd—the editor of *Further*, you know—are hand and glove. And considering he has a wife and she a husband ... well, it seems pretty futile, doesn't it?"

"Does it?" Eddy wondered. "It depends so much on the special circumstances. If the husband and the wife don't mind——"

"Rot," said James. "And the husband ought to mind, and I don't know that the wife doesn't. And, anyhow, it doesn't affect the question of right and wrong."

That was too difficult a proposition for Eddy to consider; he gave it up.

"I'm going to the Blackfriars Road flat with Denison one day, I believe," he said. "I shall be one of the Fabians that sit on the bed that doesn't look like a sofa."

James sighed. "I wish, if you get to know Sally at all, you'd encourage her to come down here more, and try to put a few sound ideas into her head. She's taking to scorning my words of wisdom. I believe she's taken against parsons.... Oh, you're going with Denison."

"Arnold won't do anyone any harm," Eddy reassured him. "He's so extraordinarily innocent. About the most innocent person I know. We should shock him frightfully down here if he saw much of us; he'd think us indecent and coarse. Hillier and I did shock him rather, by liking "The Penitent."

"I wonder if you like everything," grumbled Peters.

"Most things, I expect," said Eddy. "Well, most things are rather nice, don't you think?"

"I suppose you'll like the Le Moines and Miss Dawn if you get to know them. And all the rest of that crew."

Eddy certainly expected to do so.

Six o'clock struck, and Peters went to church to hear confessions, and Eddy to the Institute to play billiards with the Church Lads' Brigade, of which he was an officer. A wonderful life of varied active service, this Southwark life seemed to Eddy; full and splendid, and gloriously single-eyed. Arnold, in sneering at it, showed himself a narrow prig. More and more it was becoming clear to Eddy that nothing should be sneered at and nothing condemned, not the Catholic Church, nor the Salvation Army, nor the views of artists, Fabians, and Le Moines, without collars and without morals.

CHAPTER III.

PLEASANCE COURT.

ONE evening Arnold took Eddy to supper with his cousin Jane Dawn and James Peters' cousin Sally. They lived in Pleasance Court, a small square with a garden. After supper they were all going to a first performance of a play by Cecil Le Moine, called "Squibs."

"You always know which their window is," Arnold told Eddy as they turned into the square, "by the things on the sill. They put the food and drink there, to keep cool, or be out of the way, or something." Looking up, they saw outside an upper window a blue jug and a white bowl, keeping cool in the moonlight. As they rang at the door, the window was pushed up, and hands reached out to take the jug and bowl in. A cheerful face looked down at the tops of their heads, and a cheerful voice said clearly,

"They've come, Jane. They're very early, aren't they? They'll have to help buttering the eggs."

Arnold called up, "If you would prefer it, we will walk round the square till the eggs are buttered."

"Oh, no, please. We'd like you to come up and help, if you don't mind." The voice was a little doubtful because of Eddy, the unknown quantity. The door was opened by an aged door-keeper, and they climbed breathlessly steep stairs to the room.

In the room was the smell of eggs buttering over a spirit-lamp, and of cocoa boiling over a fire. There was also a supper-table, laid with cups and plates and oranges and butter and honey, and brown, green-wainscotted walls, and various sorts of pictures hanging on them, and various sorts of pots and jugs from various sorts of places, such as Spain, New Brighton, and Bruges, and bronze chrysanthemums in jars, and white shoots of bulbs pricking up out of cocoa-nut fibre in bowls, and a book-case with books in it, and a table in a corner littered with book-binding plant, and two girls cooking. One of them was soft and round like a puppy, and had fluffy golden hair and a cornflower-blue pinafore to match cornflower-blue eyes. The other was small, and had a pale, pointed face and a large forehead and brown hair waving back from it, and a smile of wonderfully appealing sweetness, and a small, gentle voice. She looked somehow as if she had lived in a wood, and had intimately and affectionately known all the little live wild things in it, both birds and beasts and flowers: a queer unearthliness there was about her, that suggested the morning winds and the evening stars. Eddy, who knew some of her drawings, had noted that chaste, elfin quality in them; he was rather pleased to find it meet him so obviously in her face and bearing. Seeing the two girls, he was disposed to echo James Peters' comment, "Can't think how she and Sally made friends," and to set it down tritely to that law of contrasts which some people, in the teeth of experience, appear to believe in as the best basis of friendship.

Sally Peters was stirring the buttered egg vigorously, lest it should stand still and burn. Jane Dawn was watching the cocoa, lest it should run over and burn. Arnold wandered round the room peering at the pictures—mostly drawings and etchings—

with his near-sighted eyes, to see if there was anything new. Jane had earned a little money lately, so there were two new Duncan Grants and a Muirhead Bone, which he examined with critical approval.

"You've still got this up," he remarked, tapping Beardsley's "Ave Atque Vale" with a disparaging finger. "The one banal thing Beardsley ever.... Besides, anyhow Beardsley's *passé.*"

Jane Dawn, who looked as if she belonged not to time at all, seemed peacefully undisturbed by this fact. Only Sally, in her young ingenuousness, looked a little concerned.

"I love the Ave," Jane murmured over the saucepan, and then looked up at Eddy with her small, half-affectionate smile—a likeable way she had with her.

He said, "I do too," and Arnold snorted.

"You don't know him yet, Jane. He loves everything. He loves 'Soap-bubbles,' and 'The Monarch of the Glen,' and problem pictures in the Academy. Not to mention 'The Penitent,' which, Jane, is a play of which you have never heard, but to which you and I will one day go, to complete our education. Only we won't take Sally; it would be bad for her. She isn't old enough for it yet and it might upset her mind; besides, it isn't proper, I believe."

"I'm sure I don't want to go," said Sally, pouring out the egg into a dish. "It must be idiotic. Even Jimmy thinks so."

Arnold's eyebrows went up. "In that case I may revise my opinion of it," he murmured. "Well, anyhow Eddy loves it, like everything else. Nothing is beyond the limit of his tolerance."

"Does he like nice things too?" Sally naïvely asked. "Will he like 'Squibs'?"

"Oh, yes, he'll like 'Squibs.' His taste is catholic; he'll probably be the only person in London who likes both 'Squibs' and 'The Penitent.' ... I suppose we shan't see Eileen to-night; she'll have been given one of the seats of the great. She shall come and talk to us between the acts, though."

"We wanted Eileen and Bridget to come to supper," said Sally. "It's quite ready now, by the way; let's have it. But they were dining with Cecil, and then going on to the theatre. Do you like cocoa, Mr. Oliver? Because if you don't there's milk, or lemonade."

Eddy said he liked them all, but would have cocoa at the moment. Jane poured it out, with the most exquisitely-shaped thin small hands he had ever seen, and passed it to him with her little smile, that seemed to take him at once into the circle of her accepted friends. A rare and delicate personality she seemed to him, curiously old and young, affectionate and aloof, like a spring morning on a hill. There was something impersonal and sexless about her. Eddy felt inclined at once to call her Jane, and was amused and pleased when she slipped unconsciously once or twice into addressing him as Eddy. The ordinary conventions in such matters would never, one felt, weigh with her at all, or even come into consideration, any more than with a child.

"I was to give you James' love," Eddy said to Sally, "and ask you when you are coming to St. Gregory's again. The school-teachers, he tells me to inform you, cannot run the Band of Hope basket-making class without you."

Sally got rather pink, and glanced at Arnold, who looked cynically interested.

"What *is* the Band of Hope?" he inquired.

"Temperance girls, temperance boys, always happy, always free," Eddy answered, in the words of their own song.

"Oh, I see. Fight the drink. And does making baskets help them to fight it?"

"Well, of course if you have a club and it has to meet once a week, it must do something," said Sally, stating a profound and sad truth. "But I told Jimmy I was frightfully busy; I don't think I can go, really.... I wish Jimmy wouldn't go on asking me. Do tell him not to, Mr. Oliver. Jimmy doesn't understand; one can't do everything."

"No," said Eddy dubiously, thinking that perhaps one could, almost, and that anyhow the more things the more fun.

"It's a pity one can't," he added, from his heart.

Arnold said that doing was a deadly thing, doing ends in death. "Only that, I believe, is the Evangelical view, and you're High Church at St. Gregory's."

Jane laughed at him. "Imagine Arnold knowing the difference! I don't believe he does in the least. I do," she added, with a naïve touch of vanity, "because I met a clergyman once, when I was drawing in the Abbey, and he told me a lot about it. About candles, and ornaments, and robes that priests wear in church. It must be much nicer than being Low Church, I should think." She referred to Eddy, with her questioning smile.

"They're both rather nice," Eddy said. "I'm both, I think."

Sally looked at him inquiringly with her blue eyes under their thick black lashes. Was he advanced, this plausible, intelligent-looking young man, who was a friend of Arnold Denison's and liked "The Penitent," and, indeed, everything else? Was he free and progressive and on the side of the right things, or was he merely an amiable stick-in-the-mud like Jimmy? She couldn't gather, from his alert, expressive face and bright hazel eyes and rather sensitive mouth: they chiefly conveyed a capacity for reception, an openness to all impressions, a readiness to spread sails to any wind. If he *were* a person of parts, if he had a brain and a mind and a soul, and if at the same time he were an ardent server of the Church—that, Sally thought unconsciously, might be a witness in the Church's favour. Only here she remembered Jimmy's friend at St. Gregory's, Bob Traherne; he was all that and more, he had brain and mind and soul and an ardent fire of zeal for many of the right things (Sally, a little behind the times here, was a Socialist by conviction), and yet in spite of him one was sure that somehow the Church wouldn't do, wouldn't meet all the requirements of this complex life. Sally had learnt that lately, and was learning it more and more. She was proud of having learnt it; but still, she had occasional regrets.

She made a hole in an orange, and put a lump of sugar in it and sucked it.

"The great advantage of that way," she explained, "is that all the juice goes inside you, and doesn't mess the plates or anything else. You see, Mrs. Jones is rather old, and not fond of washing up."

So they all made holes and put in sugar, and put the juice inside them. Then Jane and Sally retired to exchange their cooking pinafores for out-door things, and then they all rode to "Squibs" on the top of a bus. They were joined at the pit door by one Billy Raymond, a friend of theirs—a tall, tranquil young man, by trade a poet, with an attractive smile and a sweet temper, and a gentle, kind, serenely philosophical view of men and things that was a little like Jane's, only more human and virile. He attracted Eddy greatly, as his poems had already done.

To remove anxiety on the subject, it may be stated at once that the first night of "Squibs" was neither a failure nor a triumphant success. It was enjoyable, for those who enjoyed the sort of thing—(fantastic wit, clever dialogue, much talk, little action, and less emotion)—and dull for those who didn't. It would certainly never be popular, and probably the author would have been shocked and grieved if it had been. The critics approved it as clever, and said it was rather lengthy and highly improbable. Jane, Sally, Arnold, Billy Raymond, and Eddy enjoyed it extremely. So did Eileen Le Moine and her companion Bridget Hogan, who watched it from a box. Cecil Le Moine wandered in and out of the box, looking plaintive. He told Eileen that they were doing it even worse than he had feared. He was rather an engaging-looking person, with a boyish, young-Napoleonic beauty of face and a velvet smoking-jacket, and a sweet, plaintive voice, and the air of an injured child about him. A child of genius, perhaps; anyhow a gifted child, and a lovable one, and at the same time as selfish as even a child can be.

Eileen Le Moine and Miss Hogan came to speak to their friends in the pit before taking their seats. Eddy was introduced to them, and they talked for a minute or two. When they had gone, Sally said to him, "Isn't Eileen attractive?"

"Very," he said.

"And Bridget's a dear," added Sally, childishly boasting of her friends.

"I can imagine she would be," said Eddy. Miss Hogan had amused him during their short interview. She was older than the rest of them; she was perhaps thirty-four, and very well dressed, and with a shrewd, woman-of-the-world air that the others quite lacked, and dangling pince-nez, and ironic eyes, and a slight stutter. Eddy regretted that she was not sitting among them; her caustic comments would have added salt to the evening.

"Bridget's worldly, you know," Sally said. "She's the only one of us with money, and she goes out a lot. You see how smartly she's dressed. She's the only person I'm really friends with who's like that. She's awfully clever, too, though she doesn't do anything."

"Doesn't she do anything?" Eddy asked sceptically, and Arnold answered him.

"Our Bridget? Sally only means she's a lily of the field. She writes not, neither does she paint. She only mothers those who do, and hauls them out of scrapes. Eileen lives with her, you know, in a flat in Kensington. She tries to look after Eileen. Quite enough of a job, besides tending all the other ingenuous young persons of both sexes she has under her wing."

Eddy watched her as she talked to Eileen Le Moine; a vivid, impatient, alive person, full of quips and cranks and quiddities and a constant flow of words. He could see, foreshortened, Eileen Le Moine's face—very attractive, as Sally had said; broad brows below dark hair, rounded cheeks with deep dimples that came and went in them, great deep blue, black-lashed eyes, a wide mouth of soft, generous curves, a mouth that could look sulky but always had amusement lurking in it, and a round, decisive chin. She was perhaps four or five and twenty; a brilliant, perverse young person, full of the fun of living, an artist, a pleasure-lover, a spoilt child, who probably could be sullen, who certainly was wayward and self-willed, who had genius and charm and ideas and a sublime independence of other people's codes, and possibly an immense untapped spring of generous self-sacrifice. She had probably been too like Cecil Le Moine (only more than he was, every way) to live with him; each would need something more still and restful as a permanent companion. They had no doubt been well advised to part, thought Eddy, who did not agree with James Peters about that way of regarding marriage.

"Isn't Miss Carruthers ripping as Myra," whispered Sally. "Cecil wrote it for her, you know. He says there's no one else on the stage."

Jane put up a hand to silence her, because the curtain had risen.

At the end the author was called and had a good reception; on the whole "Squibs" had been a success. Eddy looked up and saw Eileen Le Moine looking pleased and smiling as they clapped her boyish-looking husband—an amused, sisterly, half ironic smile. It struck Eddy as the smile she must inevitably give Cecil, and it seemed to illumine their whole relations. She couldn't, certainly, be the least in love with him, and yet she must like him very much, to smile like that now that they were parted.

As Jane and Sally and Eddy and Billy Raymond rode down Holborn on their bus (Arnold had walked to Soho, where he lived) Eddy, sitting next Jane, asked "Did you like it?" being curious about Jane's point of view.

She smiled. "Yes, of course. Wouldn't anyone?" Eddy could have answered the question, instancing Hillier or James Peters, or his own parents or, indeed, many other critics. But Jane's "anyone" he surmised to have a narrow meaning; anyone, she meant, of our friends; anyone of the sort one naturally comes into contact with. (Jane's outlook was through a narrow gate on to woods unviolated by the common tourist; her experience was delicate, exquisite, and limited).

She added, "Of course it's just a baby's thing. He *is* just a baby, you know."

"I should like to get to know him," said Eddy. "He's extraordinarily pleasing," and she nodded.

"Of course you'll get to know him. Why not? And Eileen, too." In Jane's world, the admitted dwellers all got to know each other, as a matter of course.

"A lot of us are going down into the country next Sunday," Jane added. "Won't you come?"

"Oh, thanks; if I'm not needed in the parish I'd love to. Yes, I'm almost sure I can."

"We all meet at Waterloo for the nine-thirty. We shall have breakfast at Heathermere (but you can have had some earlier, too, if you like), and then walk somewhere from there. Bring a thick coat, because we shall be sitting about on the heath, and it's not warm."

"Thanks awfully, if you're sure I may come."

Jane wasted no more words on that; she probably never asked people to come unless she was sure they might. She merely waved an appreciative hand, like a child, at the blue night full of lights, seeking his sympathy in the wonder of it. Then she and Sally had to change into the Blackfriars Bridge bus, and Eddy sought London Bridge and the Borough on foot. Billy Raymond, who lived in Beaufort Street, but was taking a walk, came with him. They talked on the way about the play. Billy made criticisms and comments that seemed to Eddy very much to the point, though they wouldn't have occurred to him. There was an easy ability, a serene independence of outlook, about this young man, that was attractive. Like many poets, he was singularly fresh and unspoilt, though in his case (unlike many poets) it wasn't because he had nothing to spoil him; he enjoyed, in fact, some reputation among critics and the literary public. He figured in many an anthology of verse, and those who gave addresses on modern poetry were apt to read his things aloud, which habit annoys some poets and gratifies others. Further, he had been given a reading all to himself at the Poetry Bookshop, which had rather displeased him, because he had not liked the voice of the lady who read him. But enough has been said to indicate that he was a promising young poet.

When Eddy got in, he found the vicar and Hillier smoking by the common-room fire. The vicar was nodding over Pickwick, and Hillier perusing the *Church Times*. The vicar, who had been asleep, said, "Hullo, Oliver. Want anything to eat or drink? Had a nice evening?"

"Very, thanks. No, I've been fed sufficiently."

"Play good?"

"Yes, quite clever.... I say, would it be awfully inconvenient if I was to be out next Sunday? Some people want me to go out for the day with them. Of course there's my class. But perhaps Wilkes.... He said he wouldn't mind, sometimes."

"No; that'll be all right. Speak to Wilkes, will you.... Shall you be away all day?"

"I expect so," said Eddy, feeling that Hillier looked at him askance, though the vicar didn't. Probably Hillier didn't approve of Sunday outings, thought one should be in church.

He sat down and began to talk about "Squibs."

Hillier said presently, "He's surely rather a mountebank, that Le Moine? Full of cheap sneers and clap-trap, isn't he?"

"Oh, no," said Eddy. "Certainly not clap-trap. He's very genuine, I should say; expresses his personality a good deal more successfully than most play writers."

"Oh, no doubt," Hillier said. "It's his personality, I should fancy, that's wrong."

Eddy said, "He's delightful," rather warmly, and the vicar said, "Well, now, I'm going to bed," and went, and Eddy went, too, because he didn't want to argue with Hillier, a difficult feat, and no satisfaction when achieved.

CHAPTER IV.

HEATHERMERE.

SUNDAY was the last day but one of October. They all met at Waterloo in a horrid fog, and missed the nine-thirty because Cecil Le Moine was late. He sauntered up at 9.45, tranquil and at ease, the MS. of his newest play under his arm (he obviously thought to read it to them in the course of the day—"which must be prevented," Arnold remarked). So they caught a leisured train at 9.53, and got out of it at a little white station about 10.20, and the fog was left behind, and a pure blue October sky arched over a golden and purple earth, and the air was like iced wine, thin and cool and thrilling, and tasting of heather and pinewoods. They went first to the village inn, on the edge of the woods, where they had ordered breakfast for eight. Their main object at breakfast was to ply Cecil with food, lest in a leisure moment he should say, "What if I begin my new play to you while you eat?"

"Good taste and modesty," Arnold remarked, à propos of nothing, "are so very important. We have all achieved our little successes (if we prefer to regard them in that light, rather than to take the consensus of the unintelligent opinion of our less enlightened critics). Jane has some very well-spoken of drawings even now on view in Grafton Street, and doubtless many more in Pleasance Court. Have you brought them, or any of them, with you, Jane? No? I thought as much. Eileen last night played a violin to a crowded and breathless audience. Where is the violin to-day? She has left it at home; she does not wish to force the fact of her undoubted musical talent down our throats. Bridget has earned deserved recognition as an entertainer of the great; she has a social *cachet* that we may admire without emulation. Look at her now; her dress is simplicity itself, and she deigns to play in a wood with the humble poor. Even the pince-nez is in abeyance. Billy had a selection from his works read aloud only last week to the élite of our metropolitan poetry-lovers by a famous expert, who alluded in the most flattering terms to his youthful promise. Has he his last volume in his breast-pocket? I think not. Eddy has made a name in proficiency in vigorous sports with youths; he has taught them to box and play billiards; does he come armed with gloves and a cue? I have written an essay of some merit that I have every hope will find itself in next month's *English Review*. I am sorry to disappoint you, but I have not brought it with me. When the well-bred come out for a day of well-earned recreation, they leave behind them the insignia of their several professions. For the time being they are merely individuals, without fame and without occupation, whose one object is to enjoy what is set before them by the gods. Have some more bacon, Cecil."

Cecil started. "Have you been talking, Arnold? I'm so sorry—I missed it all. I expect it was good, wasn't it?"

"No one is deceived," Arnold said, severely. "Your ingenuous air, my young friend, is overdone."

Cecil was looking at him earnestly. Eileen said, "He's wondering was it you that reviewed 'Squibs' in *Poetry and Drama*, Arnold. He always looks like that when he's thinking about reviews."

"The same phrases," Cecil murmured—"(meant to be witty, you know)—that Arnold used when commenting on 'Squibs' in private life to me. Either he used them again afterwards, feeling proud of them, to the reviewer (possibly Billy?) or the reviewer had just used them to him before he met me, and he cribbed them, or.... But I won't ask. I mustn't know. I prefer not to know. I will preserve our friendship intact."

"What does the conceited child expect?" exclaimed Miss Hogan. "The review said he was more alive than Barker, and wittier than Wilde. The grossest flattery I ever read!"

"A bright piece," Cecil remarked. "He said it was a bright piece. He did, I tell you. *A bright piece.*"

"Well, lots of the papers didn't," said Sally, consoling him. "The *Daily Comment* said it was long-winded, incoherent, and dull."

"Thank you, Sally. That is certainly a cheering memory. To be found bright by the *Daily Comment* would indeed be the last stage of degradation.... I wonder what idiocy they will find to say of my next.... I wonder——"

"Have we all finished eating?" Arnold hastily intercepted. "Then let us pay, and go out for a country stroll, to get an appetite for lunch, which will very shortly be upon us."

"My dear Arnold, one doesn't stroll immediately after breakfast; how crude you are. One smokes a cigarette first."

"Well, catch us up when you've smoked it. We came out for a day in the country, and we must have it. We're going to walk several miles now without a stop, to get warm." Arnold was occasionally seized with a fierce attack of energy, and would walk all through a day, or more probably a night, to get rid of it, and return cured for the time being.

The sandy road led first through a wood that sang in a fresh wind. The cool air was sweet with pines and bracken and damp earth. It was a glorious morning of odours and joy, and the hilarity of the last days of October, when the end seems near and the present poignantly gay, and life a bright piece nearly played out. Arnold and Bridget Hogan walked on together ahead, both talking at once, probably competing as to which could get in most remarks in the shortest time. After them came Billy Raymond and Cecil Le Moine, and with them Jane and Sally hand-in-hand. Eddy found himself walking in the rear side by side with Eileen Le Moine.

Eileen, who was capable, ignoring all polite conventions, of walking a mile with a slight acquaintance without uttering a word, because she was feeling lazy, or thinking of something interesting, or because her companion bored her, was just now in a conversational mood. She rather liked Eddy; also she saw in him an avenue for an idea she had in mind. She told him so.

"You work in the Borough, don't you? I wish you'd let me come and play folk-music to your clubs sometimes. It's a thing I'm rather keen on—getting the old folk melodies into the streets, do you see, the way errand boys will whistle them. Do you know Hugh Datcherd? He has musical evenings in his Lea-side settlement; I go there a good deal. He has morris dancing twice a week and folk-music once."

Eddy had heard much of Hugh Datcherd's Lea-side settlement. According to St. Gregory's, it was run on very regrettable lines. Hillier said, "They teach rank atheism there." However, it was something that they also taught morris dancing and folk-music.

"It would be splendid if you'd come sometimes," he said, gratefully. "Just exactly what we should most like. We've had a little morris dancing, of course—who hasn't?—but none of the other thing."

"Which evening will I come?" she asked. A direct young person; she liked to settle things quickly.

Eddy, consulting his little book, said, "To-morrow, can you?"

She said, "No, I can't; but I will," having apparently a high-handed method of dealing with previous engagements.

"It's the C.L.B. club night," said Eddy. "Hillier—one of the curates—is taking it to-morrow, and I'm helping. I'll speak to him, but I'm sure it will be all right. It will be a delightful change from billiards and boxing. Thanks so much."

"And Mr. Datcherd may come with me, mayn't he? He's interested in other people's clubs. Do you read *Further*? And do you like his books?"

"Yes, rather," Eddy comprehensively answered all three questions. All the same he was smitten with a faint doubt as to Mr. Datcherd's coming. Probably Hillier's answer to the three questions would have been "Certainly not." But after all, St. Gregory's didn't belong to Hillier but to the vicar, and the vicar was a man of sense. And anyhow anyone who saw Mrs. Le Moine must be glad to have a visit from her, and anyone who heard her play must thank the gods for it.

"I do like his books," Eddy amplified; "only they're so awfully sad, and so at odds with life."

A faint shadow seemed to cloud her face.

"He *is* awfully sad," she said, after a moment. "And he is at odds with life. He feels it hideous, and he minds. He spends all his time trying and trying can he change it for people. And the more he tries and fails, the more he minds." She stopped abruptly, as if she had gone too far in explaining Hugh Datcherd to him. Eddy had a knack of drawing confidences; probably it was his look of intelligent sympathy and his habit of listening.

He wondered for a moment whether Hugh Datcherd's sadness was all altruistic, or did he find his own life hideous too? From what Eddy had heard of Lady Dorothy, his wife, that might easily be so, he thought, for they didn't sound compatible.

Instinctively, anyhow, he turned away his eyes from the queer, soft look of brooding pity that momentarily shadowed Hugh Datcherd's friend.

From in front, snatches of talk floated back to them through the clear, thin air. Miss Hogan's voice, with its slight stutter, seemed to be concluding an interesting anecdote.

"And so they both committed suicide from the library window. And his wife was paralysed from the waist up—is still, in fact. *Most* unwholesome, it all was. And now it's so on Charles Harker's mind that he writes novels about nothing else, poor creature. Very natural, if you think what he went through. I hear he's another just coming out now, on the same."

"He sent it to us," said Arnold, "but Uncle Wilfred and I weren't sure it was proper. I am engaged in trying to broaden Uncle Wilfred's mind. Not that I want him to take Harker's books, now or at any time.... You know, I want Eddy in our business. We want a new reader, and it would be so much better for his mind and moral nature than messing about as he's doing now."

Cecil was saying to Billy and Jane, "He wants me to put Lesbia behind the window-curtain, and make her overhear it all. Behind the window-curtain, you know! He really does. Could you have suspected even our Musgrave of being so banal, Billy? He's not even Edwardian—he's late-Victorian...."

Arnold said over his shoulder, "Can't somebody stop him? Do try, Jane. He's spoiling our day with his egotistic babbling. Bridget and I are talking exclusively about others, their domestic tragedies, their literary productions, and their unsuitable careers;

never a word about ourselves. I'm sure Eileen and Eddy are doing the same; and sandwiched between us, Cecil flows on fluently about his private grievances and his highly unsuitable plays. You'd think he might remember what day it is, to say the least of it. I wonder how he was brought up, don't you, Bridget?"

"I don't wonder; I know," said Bridget. "His parents not only wrote for the Yellow Book, but gave it him to read in the nursery, and it corrupted him for life. He would, of course, faint if one suggested that he carried the taint of anything so antiquated, but infant impressions are hard to eradicate. I know of old that the only way to stop him is to feed him, so let's have lunch, however unsuitable the hour and the place may be."

Sally said, "Hurrah, let's. In this sand-pit." So they got into the sand-pit and produced seven packets of food, which is to say that they each produced one except Cecil, who had omitted to bring his, and undemurringly accepted a little bit of everyone else's. They then played hide and seek, dumb crambo, and other vigorous games, because as Arnold said, "A moment's pause, and we are undone," until for weariness the pause came upon them, and then Cecil promptly seized the moment and produced the play, and they had to listen. Arnold succumbed, vanquished, and stretched himself on the heather.

"You have won; I give in. Only leave out the parts that are least suitable for Sally to hear."

So, like other days in the country, the day wore through, and they caught the 5.10 back to Waterloo.

At supper that evening Eddy told the vicar about Mrs. Le Moine's proposal.

"So she's coming to-morrow night, with Datcherd."

Hillier looked up sharply.

"Datcherd! That man!" He caught himself up from a scornful epithet.

"Why not?" said the vicar tolerantly. "He's very keen on social work, you know."

Peters and Hillier both looked cross.

"I know personally," said Hillier, "of cases where his influence has been ruinous."

Peters said, "What does he want down here?"

Eddy said, "He won't have much influence during one evening. I suppose he wants to watch how they take the music, and, generally, to see what our clubs are like. Besides, he and Mrs. Le Moine are great friends, and she naturally likes to have someone to come with."

"Datcherd's a tremendously interesting person," said Traherne. "I've met him once or twice; I should like to see more of him."

"A very able man," said the vicar, and said grace.

CHAPTER V.

DATCHERD AND THE VICAR.

DATCHERD looked ill; that was the predominant impression Eddy got of him. An untidy, pale, sad-eyed person of thirty-five, with a bad temper and an extraordinarily ardent fire of energy, at once determined and rather hopeless. The evils of the world loomed, it seemed, even larger in his eyes than their possible remedies; but both loomed large. He was a pessimist and a reformer, an untiring fighter against overwhelming odds. He was allied both by birth and marriage (the marriage had been a by-gone mistake of the emotions, for which he was dearly paying) with a class which, without intermission, and by the mere fact of its existence, incurred his vindictive wrath. (See *Further*, month by month.) He had tried and failed to get into Parliament; he had now given up hopes of that field of energy, and was devoting himself to philanthropic social schemes and literary work. He was not an attractive person, exactly; he lacked the light touch, and the ordinary human amenities; but there was a drawing-power in the impetuous ardour of his convictions and purposes, in his acute and brilliant intelligence, in his immense, quixotic generosity, and, to some natures, in his unhappiness and his ill-health. And his smile, which came seldom, would have softened any heart.

Perhaps he did not smile at Hillier on Monday evening; anyhow Hillier's heart remained hard towards him, and his towards Hillier. He was one of the generation who left the universities fifteen years ago; they are often pronounced and thoughtful agnostics, who have thoroughly gone into the subject of Christianity as taught by the Churches, and decided against it. They have not the modern way of rejection, which is to let it alone as an irrelevant thing, a thing known (and perhaps cared) too little about to pronounce upon; or the modern way of acceptance, which is to embark upon it as an inspiring and desirable adventure. They of that old generation think that religion should be squared with science, and, if it can't be, rejected finally. Anyhow Datcherd thought so; he had rejected it finally as a Cambridge undergraduate, and had not changed his mind since. He believed freedom of thought to be of immense importance, and, a dogmatic person himself, was anxious to free the world from the fetters of dogma. Hillier (also a dogmatic person; there are so many) preached a sermon the Sunday after he had met Datcherd about those who would find themselves fools at the Judgment Day. Further, Hillier agreed with James Peters that the relations of Datcherd and Mrs. Le Moine were unfitting, considering that everyone knew that Datcherd didn't get on with his wife nor Mrs. Le Moine live with her husband. People in either of those unfortunate positions cannot be too careful of appearances.

Meanwhile, Mrs. Le Moine's fiddling held the club spell-bound. She played English folk-melodies and Hungarian dances, and the boys' feet shuffled in tune. Londoners are musical people, on the whole; no one can say that, though they like bad music, they don't like good music, too; they are catholic in taste. Eddy Oliver, who liked anything he heard, from a barrel-organ to a Beethoven Symphony, was a typical specimen. His foot, too, tapped in tune; his blood danced in him to the lilt of laughter and passion and gay living that the quick bow tore from the strings. He knew enough, technically, about music, to know that this was wonderful playing; and he remembered what he had heard before, that this brilliant, perverse, childlike-looking person, with her great brooding eyes and half-sullen brows, and the fiddle tucked away under her round chin, was a genius. He believed he had heard that she had some Hungarian blood in her, besides the Irish strain. Certainly the passion and the fire in her, that was setting everyone's blood stirring so, could hardly be merely English.

At the end of a wild dance tune, and during riotous applause, Eddy turned to Datcherd, who stood close to him, and laughed.

"My word!" was all he said.

Datcherd smiled a little at him, and Eddy liked him more than ever.

"They like it, don't they?" said Datcherd. "Look how they like it. They like this; and then we go and give them husks; vulgarities from the comic operas."

"Oh, but they like those, too," said Eddy.

Datcherd said impatiently, "They'd stop liking them if they could always get anything decent."

"But surely," said Eddy, "the more things they like the better."

Datcherd, looking round at him to see if he meant it, said, "Good heavens!" and was frowningly silent.

An intolerant man, and ill-tempered at that, Eddy decided, but liked him very much all the same.

Mrs. Le Moine was playing again, quite differently; all the passion and the wildness were gone now; she was playing a sixteenth century tune, curiously naïf and tender and engaging, and objective, like a child's singing, or Jane Dawn's drawings. The detachment of it, the utter self-obliteration, pleased Eddy even more than the passion of the dance; here was genius at its highest. It seemed to him very wonderful that she should be giving of her best so lavishly to a roomful of ignorant Borough lads; very wonderful, and at the same time very characteristic of her wayward, quixotic, self-pleasing generosity, that he fancied was neither based on any principle, nor restrained by any considerations of prudence. She would always, he imagined, give just what she felt inclined, and when she felt inclined, whatever the gifts she dealt in. Anyhow she had become immensely popular in the club-room. The admiration roused by her music was increased by the queer charm she carried with her. She stood about among the boys for a little, talking. She told them about the tunes, what they were and whence they came; she whistled a bar here and there, and they took it up from her; she had asked which they had liked, and why.

"In my Settlement up by the Lea," said Datcherd to Eddy, "she's got some of the tunes out into the streets already. You hear them being whistled as the men go to work."

Eddy looked at Hillier, to see if he hadn't been softened by this wonderful evening. Hillier, of course, had liked the music; anyone would. But his moral sense had a fine power of holding itself severely aloof from conversion by any but moral suasions. He was genially chatting with the boys, as usual—Hillier was delightful with boys and girls, and immensely popular—but Eddy suspected him unchanged in his attitude towards the visitors. Eddy, for music like that, would have loved a Mrs. Pendennis (had she been capable of producing it) let alone anyone so likeable as Eileen Le Moine. Hillier, less susceptible to influence, still sat in judgment.

Flushed and bright-eyed, Eddy made his way to Mrs. Le Moine.

"I say, thanks most awfully," he said. "I knew it was going to be wonderful, but I didn't know how wonderful. I shall come to all your concerts now."

Hillier overheard that, and his brows rose a little. He didn't see how Eddy was going to make the time to attend all Mrs. Le Moine's concerts; it would mean missing club nights, and whole afternoons. In his opinion, Eddy, for a parish worker, went too much out of the parish already.

Mrs. Le Moine said, with her usual lack of circumlocution, "I'll come again next Monday. Shall I? I would like to get the music thoroughly into their heads; they're keen enough to make it worth while."

Eddy said promptly, "Oh, will you really? How splendid."

Hillier, coming up to them, said courteously, "This has been extremely good of you, Mrs. Le Moine. We have all had a great treat. But you really mustn't waste more of your valuable time on our uncultivated ears. We're not worth it, I'm afraid."

Eileen looked at him with a glint of amusement in the gloomy blue shadowiness of her eyes.

"I won't come," she said, "unless you want me to, of course."

Hillier protested. "It's delightful for us, naturally—far more than we deserve. It was your time I was thinking of."

"That will be all right. I'll come, then, for half an hour, next Monday." She turned to Eddy. "Will you come to lunch with us—Miss Hogan and me, you know—next Sunday? Arnold Denison's coming, and Karl Lovinski, the violinist, and two or three other people. 3, Campden Hill Road, at 1.30."

"Thanks; I should like to."

Datcherd came up from the back of the room where he had been talking to Traherne, who had come in lately. They said goodbye, and the club took to billiards.

"Is Mr. Datcherd coming, too, next Monday?" Hillier inquired gloomily of Eddy.

"Oh, I expect so. I suppose it's less of a bore for Mrs. Le Moine not to have to come all that way alone. Besides, he's awfully interested in it all."

"A first-class man," said Traherne, who was an enthusiast, and had found in Datcherd another Socialist, though not a Church one.

Eddy and the curates walked back together later in the evening. Eddy felt vaguely jarred by Hillier to-night; probably because Hillier was, in his mind, opposing something, and that was the one thing that annoyed Eddy. Hillier was, he felt, opposing these delightful people who had provided the club with such a glorious evening, and were going to do so again next Monday; these brilliant people, who spilt their genius so lavishly before the poor and ignorant; these charming, friendly people, who had asked Eddy to lunch next Sunday.

What Hillier said was, "Shall you get Wilkes to take your class again on Sunday afternoon, Oliver?"

"Yes, I suppose so. He doesn't mind, does he? I believe he really takes it a lot better than I do."

Hillier believed so, too, and made no comment. Traherne laughed. "Wilkes! Oh, he means well, no doubt. But I wouldn't turn up on Sunday afternoon if I was going to be taught by Wilkes. What an ass you are, Oliver, going to lunch parties on Sundays."

With Traherne, work came first, and everything else, especially anything social, an immense number of lengths behind. With Eddy a number of things ran neck to neck all the time. He wouldn't, Traherne thought, a trifle contemptuously, ever accomplish much in any sphere of life at that rate.

He said to the vicar that night, "Oliver's being caught in the toils of Society, I fear. For such a keen person, he's oddly slack about sticking to his job when anything else turns up."

But Hillier said, at a separate time, "Oliver's being dragged into a frightfully unwholesome set, vicar. I hate those people; that man Datcherd is an aggressive unbeliever, you know; he does more harm, I believe, than anyone quite realises. And one hears things said, you know, about him and Mrs. Le Moine—oh, no harm, I daresay, but one has to think of the effect on the weaker brethren. And Oliver's bringing them into the parish, and I wouldn't care to answer for the effects.... It made me a little sick, I don't mind saying to you, to see Datcherd talking to the lads to-night; a word dropped here, a sneer there, and the seed is sown from which untold evil may spring. Of course, Mrs. Le Moine is a wonderful player, but that makes her influence all the more dangerous, to my mind. The lads were fascinated this evening; one saw them hanging on her words."

"I don't suppose," said the vicar, "that she, or Datcherd either, would say anything to hurt them."

Hillier caught him up sharply.

"You approve, then? You won't discourage Oliver's intimacy with them, or his bringing them into the parish?"

"Most certainly I shall, if it gets beyond a certain point. There's a mean in all things.... But it's their effect on Oliver rather than on the parish that I should be afraid of. He's got to realise that a man can't profitably have too many irons in the fire at once. If he's going perpetually to run about London seeing friends, he'll do no good as a worker. Also, it's not good for his soul to be continually with people who are unsympathetic with the Church. He's not strong enough or grown-up enough to stand it."

But Eddy had a delightful lunch on Sunday, and Wilkes took his class.

Other Sundays followed, and other week-days, and more delightful lunches, and many concerts and theatres, and expeditions into the country, and rambles about the town, and musical evenings in St. Gregory's parish, and, in general, a jolly life. Eddy loved the whole of life, including his work in St. Gregory's, which he was quite as much interested in as if it had been his exclusive occupation. Ingenuously, he would try to draw his friends into pleasures which they were by temperament and training little fitted to enjoy. For instance, he said to Datcherd and Mrs. Le Moine one day, "We've got a mission on now in the parish. There's an eight o'clock service on Monday night, so there'll be no club. I wish you'd come to the service instead; it's really good, the mission. Father Dempsey, of St. Austin's, is taking it. Have you ever heard him?"

Datcherd, in his grave, melancholy way, shook his head. Eileen smiled at Eddy, and patted his arm in the motherly manner she had for him.

"Now what do you think? No, we never have. Would we understand him if we did? I expect not, do you know. Tell us when the mission (is that what you call it? But I thought they were for blacks and Jews) is over, and I'll come again and play to the clubs. Till then, oughtn't you to be going to services every night, and I wonder ought you to be dining and theatreing with us on Thursday?"

"Oh, I can fit it in easily," said Eddy, cheerfully. "But, seriously, I do wish you'd come one night. You'd like Father Dempsey. He's an extraordinarily alive and stimulating person. Hillier thinks him flippant; but that's rubbish. He's the best man in the Church."

All the same, they didn't come. How difficult it is to make people do what they are not used to! How good it would be for them if they would; if Hillier would but sometimes spend an evening at Datcherd's settlement; if James Peters would but come, at Eddy's request, to shop at the Poetry Bookshop; if Datcherd would but sit under Father Dempsey, the best man in the Church! It sometimes seemed to Eddy that it was he alone, in a strange, uneclectic world, who did all these things with impartial assiduity and fervour.

And he found, which was sad and bewildering, that those with less impartiality of taste got annoyed with him. The vicar thought, not unnaturally, that during the mission he ought to have given up other engagements, and devoted himself exclusively to the parish, getting them to come. All the curates thought so too. Meanwhile Arnold Denison thought that he ought to have stayed to the end of the debate on Impressionism in Poetry at the Wednesday Club that met in Billy Raymond's rooms, instead of going away in the middle to be in time for the late service at St. Gregory's. Arnold thought so particularly because he hadn't yet spoken himself, and it would obviously have been more becoming in Eddy to wait and hear him. Eddy grew to have an uncomfortable feeling of being a little wrong with everyone; he felt aggrieved under it.

At last, a fortnight before Christmas, the vicar spoke to him. It was on a Sunday evening. Eddy had had supper with Cecil Le Moine, as it was Cecil's turn to have the Sunday Games Club, a childish institution that flourished just then among them, meet at his house. Eddy returned to St. Gregory's late.

The vicar said, at bedtime, "I want to speak to you, Oliver, if you can spare a minute or two," and they went into his study. Eddy felt rather like a schoolboy awaiting a jawing. He watched the vicar's square, sensible, kind face, through a cloud of smoke, and saw his point of view precisely. He wanted certain work done. He didn't think the work was so well done if a hundred other things were done also. He believed in certain things. He didn't think belief in those things could be quite thorough if those who held it had constant and unnecessary traffic with those who quite definitely didn't. Well, it was of course a point of view; Eddy realised that.

The vicar said, "I don't want to be interfering, Oliver. But, frankly, are you as keen on this job as you were two months ago?"

"Yes, rather," said Eddy. "Keener, I think. One gets into it, you see."

The vicar nodded, patient and a little cynical.

"Quite. Well, it's a full man's job, you know; one can't take it easy. One's got to put every bit of oneself into it, and even so there isn't near enough of most of us to get upsides with it.... Oh, I don't mean don't take on times, or don't have outside interests and plenty of friends; of course I don't. But one's got not to fritter and squander one's energies. And one's got to have one's whole heart in the work, or it doesn't get done as it should. It's a job for the keen; for the enthusiasts; for the single-minded. Do you think, Oliver, that it's quite the job for you?"

"Yes," said Eddy, readily, though crest-fallen. "I'm keen. I'm an enthusiast. I'm——" He couldn't say single-minded, so he broke off.

"Really," he added, "I'm awfully sorry if I've scamped the work lately, and been out of the parish too much. I've tried not to, honestly—I mean I've tried to fit it all in and not scamp things."

"Fit it all in!" The vicar took him up. "Precisely. There you are. Why do you try to fit in so much more than you've properly room for? Life's limited, you see. One's got to select one thing or another."

"Oh," Eddy murmured, "what an awful thought! I want to select lots and lots of things!"

"It's greedy," said the vicar. "What's more, it's silly. You'll end by getting nothing.... And now there's another thing. Of course you choose your own friends; it's no business of mine. But you bring them a good deal into the parish, and that's my business, of course. Now, I don't want to say anything against friends of yours; still less to repeat the comments of ignorant and prejudiced people; but I expect you know the sort of things such people would say about Mr. Datcherd and Mrs. Le Moine. After all, they're both married to someone else. You'll admit that they are very reckless of public opinion, and that that's a pity." He spoke cautiously, saying less than he felt, in order not to be annoying. But Eddy flushed, and for the first time looked cross.

"Surely, if people are low-minded enough——" he began.

"That," said the vicar, "is part of one's work, to consider low minds. Besides—my dear Oliver, I don't want to be censorious—but why doesn't Mrs. Le Moine live with her husband? And why isn't Datcherd ever to be seen with his wife? And why are those two perpetually together?"

Eddy grew hotter. His hand shook a little as he took out his pipe.

"The Le Moines live apart because they prefer it. Why not? Datcherd, I presume, doesn't go about with his wife because they are hopelessly unsuited to each other in every way, and bore each other horribly. I've seen Lady Dorothy Datcherd. The thought of her and Datcherd as companions is absurd. She disapproves of all he is and does. She's a worldly, selfish woman. She goes her way and he his. Surely it's best. As for Datcherd and Mrs. Le Moine—they *aren't* perpetually together. They come down here together because they're both interested; but they're in quite different sets, really. His friends are mostly social workers, and politicians, and writers of leading articles, and contributors to the quarterlies and the political press—what are called able men you know; his own family, of course, are all that sort. Her friends are artists and actors and musicians, and poets and novelists and journalists, and casual, irresponsible people who play round and have a good time and do clever work—I mean, her set and his haven't very much to do with one another really." Eddy spoke rather eagerly, as if he was anxious to impress this on the vicar and himself.

The vicar heard him out patiently, then said, "I never said anything about sets. It's him and her I'm talking about. You won't deny they're great friends. Well, no man and woman are 'great friends' in the eyes of poor people; they're something quite different. And that's not wholesome. It starts talk. And your being hand and glove with them does no good to your influence in the parish. For one thing, Datcherd's known to be an atheist. These constant Sunday outings of yours—you're always missing church, you see, and that's a poor example. I've been spoken to about it more than once by the parents of your class-boys. They think it strange that you should be close friends with people like that."

Eddy started up. "People like that? People like Hugh Datcherd and Eileen Le Moine? Good heavens! I'm not fit to black their boots, and nor are the idiots who talk about them like that. Vulgar-mouthed lunatics!"

This was unlike Eddy; he never called people vulgar, nor despised them; that was partly why he made a good church worker. The vicar looked at him over his pipe, a little irritated in his turn. He had not reckoned on the boy being so hot about these friends of his.

"It's a clear choice," said the vicar, rather sharply. "Either you give up seeing so much of these people, and certainly give up bringing them into the parish; or—I'm very sorry, because I don't want to lose you—you must give up St. Gregory's."

Eddy stood looking on the floor, angry, unhappy, uncertain.

"It's no choice at all," he said at last. "You know I can't give them up. Why can't I have them and St. Gregory's, too? What's the inconsistency? I don't understand."

The vicar looked at him impatiently. His faculty of sympathy, usually so kind, humorous, and shrewd, had run up against one of those limiting walls that very few people who are supremely in earnest over one thing are quite without. He occasionally (really not often) said a stupid thing; he did so now.

"You don't understand? Surely it's extremely simple. You can't serve God and Mammon; that's the long and the short of it. You've got to choose which."

That, of course, was final. Eddy said, "Naturally, if it's like that, I'll leave St. Gregory's at once. That is, directly it's convenient for you that I should," he added, considerate by instinct, though angry.

The vicar turned to face him. He was bitterly disappointed.

"You mean that, Oliver? You won't give it another trial, on the lines I advise? Mind, I don't mean I want you to have no friends, no outside interests.... Look at Traherne, now; he's full of them.... I only want, for your own sake and our people's, that your heart should be in your job."

"I had better go," said Eddy, knowing it for certain. He added, "Please don't think I'm going off in a stupid huff or anything. It's not that. Of course, you've every right to speak to me as you did; but it's made my position quite clear to me. I see this isn't really my job at all. I must find another."

The vicar said, holding out his hand, "I'm very sorry, Oliver. I don't want to lose you. Think it over for a week, will you, and tell me then what you have decided. Don't be hasty over it. Remember, we've all grown fond of you here; you'll be throwing away a good deal of valuable opportunity if you leave us. I think you may be missing the best in life. But I mustn't take back what I said. It is a definite choice between two ways of life. They won't mix."

"They will, they will," said Eddy to himself, and went to bed. If the vicar thought they wouldn't, the vicar's way of life could not be his. He had no need to think it over for a week. He was going home for Christmas, and he would not come back after that. This job was not for him. And he could not, he knew now, be a clergyman. They drew lines; they objected to people and things; they failed to accept. The vicar, when he had mentioned Datcherd, had looked as Datcherd had looked when Eddy had mentioned Father Dempsey and the mission; Eddy was getting to know that critical, disapproving look too well. Everywhere it met him. He hated it. It seemed to him even stranger in clergymen than in others, because clergymen are Christians, and, to Eddy's view, there were no negations in that vivid and intensely positive creed. Its commands were always, surely, to go and do, not to abstain and reject. And look, too, at the sort of people who were of old accepted in that generous, all-embracing circle....

CHAPTER VI.

THE DEANERY AND THE HALL.

EDDY was met at the station by his sister Daphne, driving the dog-cart. Daphne was twenty; a small, neat person in tailor-made tweeds, bright-haired, with an attractive brown-tanned face, and alert blue eyes, and a decisively-cut mouth, and long, straight chin. Daphne was off-hand, quick-witted, intensely practical, spoilt, rather selfish, very sure of herself, and with an unveiled youthful contempt for manners and people that failed to meet with her approval. Either people were "all right," and "pretty decent," or they were cursorily dismissed as "queer," "messy," or "stodgy." She was very good at all games requiring activity, speed, and dexterity of hand, and more at home out of doors than in. She had quite enough sense of humour, a sharp tongue, some cleverness, and very little imagination indeed. A confident young person, determined to get and keep the best out of life. With none of Eddy's knack of seeing a number of things at once, she saw a few things very clearly, and went straight towards them.

"Hullo, young Daffy," Eddy called out to her, as he came out of the station.

She waved her whip at him.

"Hullo. I've brought the new pony along. Come and try him. He shies at cats and small children, so look out through the streets. How are you, Tedders? Pretty fit?"

"Yes, rather. How's everyone?"

"Going strong, as usual. Father talks Prayer Book revision every night at dinner till I drop asleep. He's got it fearfully hot and strong just now; meetings about it twice a week, and letters to the *Guardian* in between. I wish they'd hurry up and get it revised and have done. Oh, by the way, he says you'll want to fight him about that now—because you'll be too High to want it touched, or something. *Are* you High?"

"Oh, I think so. But I should like the Prayer Book to be revised, too."

Daphne sighed. "It's a bore if you're High. Father'll want to argue at meals. I do hope you don't want to keep the Athanasian Creed, anyhow."

"Yes, rather. I like it, except the bits slanging other people."

"Oh, well," Daphne looked relieved. "As long as you don't like those bits, I daresay it'll be all right. Canon Jackson came to lunch yesterday, and he liked it, slanging and all, and oh, my word, how tired I got of him and father! What can it matter whether one has it or not? It's only a few times a year, anyhow. Oh, and father's keen on a new translation of the Bible, too. I daresay you've seen about it; he keeps writing articles in the *Spectator* about it.... And the Bellairs have got a new car, a Panhard; Molly's learning to drive it. Nevill let me the other day; it was ripping. I do wish father'd keep a car. I should think he might now. It would be awfully useful for him for touring round to committee meetings. Mind that corner; Timothy always funks it a bit."

They turned into the drive. It may or may not have hitherto been mentioned that Eddy's home was a Deanery, because his father was a Dean. The Cathedral under his care was in a midland county, in fine, rolling, high-hedged country, suitable for hunting, and set with hard-working squires. The midlands may not be picturesque or romantic, but they are wonderfully healthy, and produce quite a number of sane, level-headed, intelligent people.

Eddy's father and mother were in the hall.

"You look a little tired, dear," said his mother, after the greetings that may be imagined. "I expect it will be good for you to get a rest at home."

"Trust Finch to keep his workers on the run," said the Dean, who had been at Cambridge with Finch, and hadn't liked him particularly. Finch had been too High Church for his taste even then; he himself had always been Broad, which was, no doubt, why he was now a dean.

"Christmas is a busy time," said Eddy, tritely.

The Dean shook his head. "They overdo it, you know, those people. Too many services, and meetings, and guilds, and I don't know what. They spoil their own work by it."

He was, naturally, anxious about Eddy. He didn't want him to get involved with the ritualist set and become that sort of parson; he thought it foolish, obscurantist, childish, and unintelligent, not to say a little unmanly.

They went into lunch. The Dean was rather vexed because Eddy, forgetting where he was, crossed himself at grace. Eddy perceived this, and registered a note not to do it again.

"And when have you to be back, dear?" said his mother. She, like many deans' wives, was a dignified, intelligent, and courteous lady, with many social claims punctually and graciously fulfilled, and a great love of breeding, nice manners, and suitable attire. She had many anxieties, finely restrained. She was anxious lest the Dean should overwork himself and get a bad throat; lest Daphne should get a tooth knocked out at mixed hockey, or a leg broken in the hunting-field; lest Eddy should choose an unsuitable career or an unsuitable wife, or very unsuitable ideas. These were her negative anxieties. Her positive ones were that the Dean should be recognised according to his merits; that Daphne should marry the right man; that Eddy should be a success, and also please his father; that the Prayer Book might be revised very soon.

One of her ambitions for Eddy was satisfied forthwith, for he pleased his father.

"I'm not going back to St. Gregory's at all."

The Dean looked up quickly.

"Oh, you've given that up, have you? Well, it couldn't go on always, of course." He wanted to ask, "What have you decided about Orders?" but, as fathers go, he was fairly tactful. Besides, he knew Daphne would.

"Are you going into the Church, Tedders?"

Her mother, as always when she put it like that, corrected her. "You know father hates you to say that, Daphne. Take Orders."

"Well, take Orders, then. Are you, Tedders?"

"I think not," said Eddy, good-tempered as brothers go. "At present I've been offered a small reviewing job on the *Daily Post*. I was rather lucky, because it's awfully hard to get on the *Post*, and, of course, I've had no experience except at Cambridge; but I know Maine, the literary editor. I used to review a good deal for the *Cambridge Weekly* when his brother ran it. I think it will be rather fun. You get such lots of nice books to keep for your own if you review."

"Nice and otherwise, no doubt," said the Dean. "You'll want to get rid of most of them, I expect. Well, reviewing is an interesting side of journalism, of course, if you are going to try journalism. You genuinely feel you want to do this, do you?"

He still had hopes that Eddy, once free of the ritualistic set, would become a Broad Church clergyman in time. But clergymen are the broader, he believed, for knocking about the world a little first.

Eddy said he did genuinely feel he wanted to do it.

"I'm rather keen to do a little writing of my own as well," he added, "and it will leave me some time for that, as well as time for other work. I want to go sometimes to work in the settlement of a man I know, too."

"What shall you write?" Daphne wanted to know.

"Oh, much what every one else writes, I suppose. I leave it to your imagination."

"H'm. Perhaps it will stay there," Daphne speculated, which was superfluously unkind, considering that Eddy used to write quite a lot at Cambridge, in the *Review*, the *Magazine*, the *Granta*, the *Basileon*, and even the *Tripod*.

"An able journalist," said the Dean, "has a great power in his hands. He can do more than the politicians to mould public opinion. It's a great responsibility. Look at the *Guardian*, now; and the *Times*."

Eddy looked at them, where they lay on the table by the window. He looked also at the *Spectator*, *Punch*, the *Morning Post*, the *Saturday Westminster*, the *Quarterly*, the *Church Quarterly*, the *Hibbert*, the *Cornhill*, the *Commonwealth*, the *Common Cause*, and *Country Life*. These were among the periodicals taken in at the Deanery. Among those not taken in were the *Clarion*, the *Eye-Witness* (as it was called in those bygone days) the *Church Times*, *Poetry and Drama*, the *Blue Review*, the *English Review*, the *Suffragette*, *Further*, and all the halfpenny dailies. All the same, it was a well-read home, and broad-minded, too, and liked to hear two sides (but not more) of a question, as will be inferred from the above list of its periodical literature.

They had coffee in the hall after lunch. Grace, ease, spaciousness, a quiet, well-bred luxury, characterised the Deanery. It was a well-marked change to Eddy, both from the asceticism of St. Gregory's, and the bohemianism (to use an idiotic, inevitable word) of many of his other London friends. This was a true gentleman's home, one of the stately homes of England, how beautiful they stand.

Daphne proposed that they should visit another that afternoon. She had to call at the Bellairs' for a puppy. Colonel Bellairs was a land-owner and J.P., whose home was two miles out of the town. His children and the Dean's children had been intimate friends since the Dean came to Welchester from Ely, where he had been a Canon, five years ago. Molly Bellairs was Daphne Oliver's greatest friend. There were also several boys, who flourished respectively in Parliament, the Army, Oxford, Eton,

and Dartmouth. They were fond of Eddy, but did not know why
he did not enter one of the Government services, which seems
the obvious thing to do.

Before starting on this expedition, Daphne and Eddy went round
the premises, as they always did on Eddy's first day at home.
They played a round of bumble-puppy on the small lawn,
inspected the new tennis court that had just been laid, and was in
danger of not lying quite flat, and visited the kennels and the
stables, where Eddy fed his horse with a carrot and examined his
legs, and discussed with the groom the prospects of hunting
weather next week, and Daphne petted the nervous Timothy,
who shied at children and cats.

These pleasing duties done, they set out briskly for the Hall,
along the field path. It was just not freezing. The air blew round
them crisp and cool and stinging, and sang in the bare beech
woods that their path skirted. Above them white clouds sailed
about a blue sky. The brown earth was full of a repressed yet
vigorous joy. Eddy and Daphne swung along quickly through
fields and lanes. Eddy felt the exuberance of the crisp weather
and the splendid earth tingle through him. It was one of the many
things he loved, and felt utterly at home with, this motion across
open country, on foot or on horse-back. Daphne, too, felt and
looked at home, with her firm, light step, and her neat, useful
stick, and her fair hair blowing in strands under her tweed hat,
and all the competent, wholesome young grace of her. Daphne
was rather charming, there was no doubt about that. It sometimes
occurred to Eddy when he met her after an absence. There was a
sort of a drawing-power about her that was quite apart from
beauty, and that made her a popular and sought-after person, in
spite of her casual manners and her frequent selfishnesses. The
young men of the neighbourhood all liked Daphne, and
consequently she had a very good time, and was decidedly
spoilt, and, in a cool, not unattractive way, rather conceited. She
seldom had any tumbles mortifying to her self-confidence, partly
because she was in general clever and competent at the things
that came in her way to do, and partly because she did not try to
do those she would have been less good at, not from any fear of
failure, but simply because she was bored by them. But a
clergyman's daughter, even a dean's, has, unfortunately, to do a

few things that bore her. One is bazaars. Another is leaving things at cottages. Mrs. Oliver had given them a brown paper parcel to leave at a house in the lane. They left it, and Eddy stayed for a moment to talk with the lady of the house. Master Eddy was generally beloved in Welchester, because he always had plenty of attention to bestow even on the poorest and dullest. Miss Daphne was beloved, too, and admired, but was usually more in a hurry. She was in a hurry to-day, and wouldn't let Eddy stay long.

"If you let Mrs. Tom Clark start on Tom's abscess, we should never get to the Hall to-day," she said, as they left the cottage. "Besides, I hate abscesses."

"But I like Tom and his wife," said Eddy.

"Oh, they're all right. The cottage is awfully stuffy, and always in a mess. I should think she might keep it cleaner, with a little perseverance and carbolic soap. Perhaps she doesn't because Miss Harris is always jawing to her about it. I wouldn't tidy up, I must say, if Miss Harris was on to me about my room. What do you think, she's gone and made mother promise I shall take the doll stall at the Assistant Curates' Bazaar. It's too bad. I'd have dressed any number of dolls, but I do bar selling them. It's a hunting day, too. It's an awful fate to be a parson's daughter. It's all right for you; parsons' sons don't have to sell dolls."

"Look here," said Eddy, "are we having people to stay after Christmas?"

"Don't think so. Only casual droppers-in here and there; Aunt Maimie and so on. Why?"

"Because, if we've room, I want to ask some people; friends of mine in London. Denison's one."

Daphne, who knew Denison slightly, and did not like him, received this without joy. They had met last year at Cambridge, and he had annoyed her in several ways. One was his clothes; Daphne liked men to be neat. Another was, that at the dance given by the college which he and Eddy adorned, he had not asked her to dance, though introduced for that purpose, but had stood at her side while she sat partnerless through her favourite waltz, apparently under the delusion that what was required of him was interesting conversation. Even that had failed before long, as Daphne had neither found it interesting nor pretended to do so, and they remained in silence together, she indignant and he unperturbed, watching the festivities with an indulgent, if cynical, eye. A disagreeable, useless, superfluous person, Daphne considered him. He gathered this; it required no great subtlety to gather things from Daphne; and accommodated himself to her idea of him, laying himself out to provoke and tease. He was one of the few people who could sting Daphne to real temper.

So she said, "Oh."

"The others," went on Eddy, hastily, "are two girls I know; they've been over-working rather and are run down, and I thought it might be rather good for them to come here. Besides, they're great friends of mine, and of Denison's—(one of them's his cousin)—and awfully nice. I've written about them sometimes, I expect—Jane Dawn and Eileen Le Moine. Jane draws extraordinarily nice things in pen and ink, and is altogether rather a refreshing person. Eileen plays the violin—you must have heard her name—Mrs. Le Moine. Everyone's going to hear her just now; she's wonderful."

"She'd better play at the bazaar, I should think," suggested Daphne, who didn't see why parsons' daughters should be the only ones involved in this bazaar business. She wasn't very fond of artists and musicians and literary people, for the most part; so often their conversation was about things that bored one.

"Are they pretty?" she inquired, wanting to know if Eddy was at all in love with either of them. It might be amusing if he was.

Eddy considered. "I don't know that you'd call Jane pretty, exactly. Very nice to look at. Sweet-looking, and extraordinarily innocent."

"I don't like sweet innocent girls," said Daphne. "They're so inept, as a rule."

"Well, Jane's very ept. She's tremendously clever at her own things, you know; in fact, clever all round, only clever's not a bit the word as a matter of fact. She's a genius, I suppose—a sort of inspired child, very simple about everything, and delightful to talk to. Not the least conventional."

"No; I didn't suppose she'd be that. And what's Mrs.—the other one like?"

"Mrs. Le Moine. Oh, well—she's—she's very nice, too."

"Pretty?"

"Rather beautiful, she is. Irish, and a little Hungarian, I believe. She plays marvellously."

"Yes, you said that."

Daphne's thoughts on Mrs. Le Moine produced the question, "Is she married, or a widow?"

"Married. She's quite friends with her husband."

"Well, I suppose she would be. Ought to be, anyhow Can we have her without him, by the way?"

"Oh, they don't live together. That's why they're friends. They weren't till they parted. Everyone asks them about separately of course. She lives with a Miss Hogan, an awfully charming person. I'd love to ask her, too, but there wouldn't be room. I wonder if mother'll mind my asking those three?"

"You'd better find out," advised Daphne. "They won't rub father the wrong way, I suppose, will they? He doesn't like being surprised, remember. You'd better warn Mr. Denison not to talk against religion or anything."

"Oh, Denison will be all right. He knows it's a Deanery."

"Will the others know it's a Deanery, too?"

Eddy, to say the truth, had a shade of doubt as to that. They were both so innocent. Arnold had learnt a little at Cambridge about the attitude of the superior clergy, and what not to say to them, though he knew more than he always practised. Jane had been at Somerville College, Oxford, but this particular branch of learning is not taught there. Eileen had never adorned any institution for the higher education. Her father was an Irish poet, and the editor of a Nationalist paper, and did not like any of the many Deans of his acquaintance. In Ireland, Deans and Nationalists do not always see eye to eye. Eddy hoped that Eileen had not any hereditary distaste for the profession.

"Father and mother'll think it funny, Mrs. Le Moine not living with her husband," said Daphne, who had that insight into her parents' minds which comes of twenty years co-residence.

Eddy was afraid they would.

"But it's not funny, really, and they'll soon see it's quite all right. They'll like her, I know. Everyone who knows her does."

He remembered as he spoke that Hillier didn't, and James Peters didn't much. But surely the Dean wouldn't be found on any point in agreement with Hillier, or even with the cheery, unthinking Peters, innocent of the Higher Criticism. Perhaps it might be diplomatic to tell the Dean that these two young clergymen didn't much like Eileen Le Moine.

While Eddy ruminated on this question, they reached the Hall. The Hall was that type of hall they erected in the days of our earlier Georges; it had risen on the site of an Elizabethan house belonging to the same family. This is mentioned in order to indicate that the Bellairs' had long been of solid worth in the country. In themselves, they were pleasant, hospitable, clean-bred, active people, of a certain charm, which those susceptible to all kinds of charm, like Eddy, felt keenly. Finally, none of them were clever, all of them were nicely dressed, and most of them were on the lawn, hitting at a captive golf-ball, which was one of the many things they did well, though it is at best an unsatisfactory occupation, achieving little in the way of showy results. They left it readily to welcome Eddy and Daphne.

Dick (the Guards) said, "Hullo, old man, home for Christmas? Good for you. Come and shoot on Wednesday, will you? Not a parson yet, then?"

Daphne said, "He's off that just now."

Eddy said, "I'm going on a paper for the present."

Claude (Magdalen) said, "A *what*? What a funny game! Shall you have to go to weddings and sit at the back and write about the bride's clothes? What a rag!"

Nevill (the House of Commons) said, "What paper?" in case it should be one on the wrong side. It may here be mentioned (what may or may not have been inferred) that the Bellairs' belonged to the Conservative party in the state. Nevill a little suspected Eddy's soundness in this matter (though he did not know that Eddy belonged to the Fabian Society as well as to the Primrose League). Also he knew well the sad fact that our Liberal organs are largely served by Conservative journalists, and our great Tory press fed by Radicals from Balliol College, Oxford, King's College, Cambridge, and many other less refined homes of sophistry. This fact Nevill rightly called disgusting. He did not think these journalists honest or good men. So he asked, "What paper?" rather suspiciously.

Eddy said, "The *Daily Post*," which is a Conservative organ, and also costs a penny, a highly respectable sum, so Nevill was relieved.

"Afraid you might be going on some Radical rag," he said, quite superfluously, as it had been obvious he had been afraid of that. "Some Unionists do. Awfully unprincipled, I call it. I can't see how they square it with themselves."

"I should think quite easily," said Eddy; but added, to avert an argument (he had tried arguing with Nevill often, and failed), "But my paper's politics won't touch me. I'm going as literary reviewer, entirely."

"Oh, I see." Nevill lost interest, because literature isn't interesting, like politics. "Novels and poetry, and all that." Novels and poetry and all that of course must be reviewed, if written; but neither the writing of them nor the reviewing (perhaps not the reading either, only that takes less time) seems quite a man's work.

Molly (the girl) said, "*I* think it's an awfully interesting plan, Eddy," though she was a little sorry Eddy wasn't going into the

Church. (The Bellairs were allowed to call it that, though Daphne wasn't.)

Molly could be relied on always to be sympathetic and nice. She was a sunny, round-faced person of twenty, with clear, amber-brown eyes and curly brown hair, and a merry infectious laugh. People thought her a dear little girl; she was so sweet-tempered, and unselfish, and charmingly polite, and at the same time full of hilarious high spirits, and happy, tomboyish energies. Though less magnetic, she was really much nicer than Daphne. The two were very fond of one another. Everyone, including her brothers and Eddy Oliver, was fond of Molly. Eddy and she had become, in the last two years, since Molly grew up, close friends.

"Well, look here," said Daphne, "we've come for the puppy," and so they all went to the yard, where the puppy lived.

The puppy was plump and playful and amber-eyed, and rather like Molly, as Eddy remarked.

"The Diddums! I wish I *was* like him," Molly returned, hugging him, while his brother and sister tumbled about her ankles. "He's rather fatter than Wasums, Daffy, but not *quite* so tubby as Babs. I thought you should have the middle one."

"He's an utter joy," said Daphne, taking him.

"Perhaps I'd better walk down the lane with you when you go," said Molly, "so as to break the parting for him. But come in to tea now, won't you."

"Shall we, Eddy?" said Daphne. "D'you think we should? There'll be canons' wives at home."

"That settles it," said Eddy. "There won't be us. Much as I like canons' wives, it's rather much on one's very first day. I have to get used to these things gradually, or I get upset. Come on, Molly, there's time for one go at bumble-puppy before tea."

They went off together, and Daphne stayed about the stables and yard with the boys and the dogs.

The Bellairs' had that immensely preferable sort of tea which takes place round a table, and has jam and knives. They didn't have this at the Deanery, because people do drop in so at Deaneries, and there mightn't be enough places laid, besides, drawing-room tea is politer to canons and their wives. So that alone would have been a reason why Daphne and Eddy liked tea with the Bellairs'. Also, the Bellairs' *en famille* were a delightful and jolly party. Colonel Bellairs was hospitable, genial, and entertaining; Mrs. Bellairs was most wonderfully kind, and rather like Molly on a sobered, motherly, and considerably filled-out scale. They were less enlightened than at the Deanery, but quite prepared to admit that the Prayer Book ought to be revised, if the Dean thought so, though for them, personally, it was good enough as it stood. There were few people so kind-hearted, so genuinely courteous and well-bred.

Colonel Bellairs, though a little sorry for the Dean because Eddy didn't seem to be settling down steadily into a sensible profession—(in his own case the "What to do with our boys" problem had always been very simple)—was fond of his friend's son, and very kind to him, and thought him a nice, attractive lad, even if he hadn't yet found himself. He and his wife both hoped that Eddy would make this discovery before long, for a reason they had.

After tea Claude and Molly started back with the Olivers, to break the parting for Diddums. Eddy wanted to tell Molly about his prospects, and for her to tell him how interesting they were (Molly was always so delightfully interested in anything one told her), so he and she walked on ahead down the lane, in the pale light of the Christmas moon, that rose soon after tea. (It was a year when this occurred).

"I expect," he said, "you think it's fairly feeble to have begun a thing and be dropping it so soon. But I suppose one has to try round a little, to find out what one's job really is."

"Why, of course. It would be absurd to stick on if it isn't really what you like to do."

"I did like it, too. Only I found I didn't want to give it quite all my time and interest. I can't be that sort of thorough, one-job man. The men there are. Traherne, now—I wish you knew him; he's splendid. He simply throws himself into it body and soul, and says no to everything else. I can't. I don't think I even want to. Life's too many-sided for that, it seems to me, and one wants to have it all—or lots of it, anyhow. The consequence was that I was chucked out. Finch told me I was to cut off those other things, or get out. So I got out. I quite see his point of view, and that he was right in a way; but I couldn't do it. He wanted me to see less of my friends, for one thing; thought they got in the way of work, which perhaps they may have sometimes; also he didn't much approve of all of them. That's so funny. Why shouldn't one be friends with anyone one can, even if their point of view isn't altogether one's own?"

"Of course." Molly considered it for a moment, and added, "I believe I could be friends with anyone, except a heathen."

"A what?"

"A heathen. An unbeliever, you know."

"Oh, I see. I thought you meant a black. Well, it partly depends on what they don't believe, of course. I think, personally, one should try to believe as many things as one can, it's more interesting; but I don't feel any barrier between me and those who believe much less. Nor would you, if you got to know them and like them. One doesn't like people for what they believe, or dislike them for what they don't believe. It simply doesn't come in at all."

All the same, Molly did not think she could be real friends with a heathen. The fact that Eddy did, very slightly worried her; she preferred to agree with Eddy. But she was always staunch to her own principles, and didn't attempt to do so in this matter.

"I want you to meet some friends of mine who I hope are coming to stay after Christmas," went on Eddy, who knew he could rely on a much more sympathetic welcome for his friends from Molly than from Daphne. "I'm sure you'll like them immensely. One's Arnold Denison, whom I expect you've heard of." (Molly had, from Daphne.) "The others are girls—Jane Dawn and Eileen Le Moine." He talked a little about Jane Dawn and Eileen

Le Moine, as he had talked to Daphne, but more fully, because Molly was a more gratifying listener.

"They sound awfully nice. So original and clever," was her comment. "It must be perfectly ripping to be able to do anything really well. I wish I could."

"So do I," said Eddy. "I love the people who can. They're so— — well, alive, somehow. Even more than most people, I mean; if possible," he added, conscious of Molly's intense aliveness, and Daphne's, and his own, and Diddums'. But the geniuses, he knew, had a sort of white-hot flame of living beyond even that....

"We'd better wait here for the others," said Molly, stopping at the field gate, "and I'll hand over Diddums to Daffy. He'll feel it's all right if I put him in her arms and tell him to stay there."

They waited, sitting on the stile. The silver light flooded the brown fields, turning them grey and pale. It silvered Diddums' absurd brown body as he snuggled in Molly's arms, and Molly's curly, escaping waves of hair and small sweet face, a little paled by its radiance. To Eddy the grey fields and woods and Molly and Diddums beneath the moon made a delightful home-like picture, of which he himself was very much part. Eddy certainly had a convenient knack of fitting into any picture without a jar, whether it was a Sunday School class at St. Gregory's, a Sunday Games Club in Chelsea, a canons' tea at the Deanery, the stables and kennels at the Hall, or a walk with a puppy over country fields. He belonged to all of them, and they to him, so that no one ever said "What is *he* doing in that *galère*?" as is said from time to time of most of us.

Eddy, as they waited for Claude and Daphne at the gate, was wondering a little whether his new friends would fit easily into this picture. He hoped so, very much.

The others came up, bickering as usual. Molly put Diddums into Daphne's arms and told him to stay there, and they parted.

CHAPTER VII.

VISITORS AT THE DEANERY.

EDDY, while they played coon-can that evening (a horrid game prevalent at this time) approached his parents on the subject of the visitors he wanted. He mentioned to them the facts already retailed to Daphne and Molly concerning their accomplishments and virtues (omitting those concerning their domestic arrangements). And these eulogies are a mistake when one is asking friends to stay. One should not utter them. To do so starts a prejudice hard to eradicate in the minds of parents and brothers and sisters, and the visit may prove a failure. Eddy was intelligent and should have known this, but he was in an unthinking mood this Christmas, and did it.

His mother kindly said, "Very well, dear. Which day do you want them to come?"

"I'd rather like them to be here for New Year's day, if you don't mind. They might come on the thirty-first."

Eddy put down three twos in the first round, for the excellent reason that he had collected them. Daphne, disgusted, said, "Look at Teddy saving six points off his damage! I suppose that's the way they play in your slum."

Mrs. Oliver said, "Very well. Remember the Bellairs' are coming to dinner on New Year's Day. It will make rather a large party, but we can manage all right."

"Your turn, mother," said Daphne, who did not like dawdling.

The Dean, who had been looking thoughtful, said, "Le Moine, did you say one of your friends was called? No relation, I suppose, to that writer Le Moine, whose play was censored not long ago?"

"Yes, that's her husband. But he's a delightful person. And it was a delightful play, too. Not a bit dull or vulgar or pompous, like some censored plays. He only put in the parts they didn't like just for fun, to see whether it would be censored or not, and partly because someone had betted him he couldn't get censored if he tried."

The Dean looked as if he thought that silly. But he did not mean to talk about censored plays, because of Daphne, who was young. So he only said, "Playing with fire," and changed the subject. "Is it raining outside, Daffy?" he inquired with humorous intention, as his turn came round to play. As no one asked him why he wanted to know, he told them. "Because, if you don't mind, I'm thinking of going out," and he laid his hand on the table.

"Oh, I say, father! Two jokers! No wonder you're out." (This jargon of an old-time but once popular game perhaps demands apology; anyhow no one need try to understand it. *Tout passe, tout lasse....* Even the Tango Tea will all too soon be out of mode).

The Dean rose from the table. "Now I must stop this frivolling. I've any amount of work to get through."

"Don't go on too long, Everard." Mrs. Oliver was afraid his head would ache.

"Needs must, I'm afraid, when a certain person drives. The certain person in this case being represented by poor old Taggert."

Poor old Taggert was connected with another Church paper, higher than the *Guardian*, and he had been writing in this paper long challenges to the Dean "to satisfactorily explain" what he had meant by certain expressions used by him in his last letter on Revision. The Dean could satisfactorily explain anything, and found it an agreeable exercise, but one that took time and energy.

"Frightful waste of time, *I* call it," said Daphne, when the door was shut. "Because they never will agree, and they don't seem to get any further by talking. Why don't they toss up or something, to see who's right? Or draw lots. Long one, revise it all, middle one, revise it as father and his lot want, short one, let it alone, like the *Church Times* and Canon Jackson want."

"Don't be silly, dear," said her mother, absently.

"Some day," added Eddy, "you may be old enough to understand these difficult things, dear. Till then, try and be seen and not heard."

"Anyhow," said Daphne, "I go out.... I believe this is rather a footling game, really. It doesn't amuse one more than a week. I'd rather play bridge, or hide and seek."

Christmas passed, as Christmas will pass, only give it time. They kept it at the deanery much as they keep it at other deaneries, and, indeed, in very many homes not deaneries. They did up parcels and ran short of brown paper, and bought more string and many more stamps, and sent off cards and cards, and received cards and cards and cards, and hurried to send off more cards to make up the difference (but some only arrived on Christmas Day, a mean trick, and had to wait to be returned till the new year), and took round parcels, and at last rested, and Christmas Day dawned. It was a bright frosty day, with ice, etcetera, and the Olivers went skating in the afternoon with the Bellairs, round and round oranges. Eddy taught Molly a new trick, or step, or whatever those who skate call what they learn, and Daphne and the Bellairs boys flew about hand-in-hand, graceful and charming to watch. In the night it snowed, and next day they all tobogganed.

"I haven't seen Molly looking so well for weeks," said Molly's mother to her father, though indeed Molly usually looked well.

"Healthy weather," said Colonel Bellairs, "and healthy exercise. I like to see all those children playing together."

His wife liked it too, and beamed on them all at tea, which the Olivers often came in to after the healthy exercise.

Meanwhile Arnold Denison and Jane Dawn and Eileen Le Moine all wrote to say they would come on the thirty-first, which they proceeded to do. They came by three different trains, and Eddy spent the afternoon meeting them, instead of skating with the Bellairs. First Arnold came, from Cambridge, and twenty minutes later Jane, from Oxford, without her bag, which she had mislaid at Rugby. Meanwhile Eddy got a long telegram from Eileen to the effect that she had missed her train and was coming by the next. He took Jane and Arnold home to tea.

Daphne was still skating. The Dean and his wife were always charming to guests. The Dean talked Cambridge to Arnold. He had been up with Professor Denison, and many other people, and had always kept in touch with Cambridge, as he remarked. Sometimes, while a canon of Ely, he had preached the University Sermon. He did not wholly approve of the social and theological, or non-theological, outlook of Professor Denison and his family; but still, the Denisons were able and interesting and respect-worthy people, if cranky. Arnold the Dean suspected of being very cranky indeed; not the friend he would have chosen for Eddy in the improbable hypothesis of his having had the selection of Eddy's friends. Certainly not the person he would have chosen for Eddy to share rooms with, as was now their plan. But nothing of this appeared in his courteous, if not very effusive, manner to his guest.

To Jane he talked about her father, a distinguished Oxford scholar, and meanwhile eyed her a little curiously, wondering why she looked somehow different from the girls he was used to. His wife could have told him it was because she had on a grey-blue dress, rather beautifully embroidered on the yoke and cuffs, instead of a shirt and coat and skirt. She was not surprised, being one of those people whose rather limited experience has taught them that artists are often like that. She talked to Jane about Welchester, and the Cathedral, and its windows, some of which were good. Jane, with her small sweet voice and pretty manners and charming, friendly smile, was bound to make a pleasant impression on anybody not too greatly prejudiced by the grey-blue dress. And Mrs. Oliver was artistic enough to see that the dress suited her, though she herself preferred that girls should not make themselves look like early Italian pictures of St. Ursula. It might be all right in Oxford or Cambridge (one understands that this style is still, though with decreasing frequency, occasionally to be met with in our older Universities), or no doubt, at Letchworth and the Hampstead Garden City, and possibly beyond Blackfriars Bridge (Mrs. Oliver was vague as to this, not knowing that part of London well); but in Welchester, a midland cathedral country town, it was unsuitable, and not done.

Mrs. Oliver wondered whether Eddy didn't mind, but he didn't seem to. Eddy had never minded the things most boys mind in those ways; he had never, when at school, betrayed the least anxiety concerning his parents' clothes or manners when they had visited him; probably he thought all clothes and all manners, like all ideas, were very nice, in their different ways.

But when Daphne came in, tweed-skirted, and clad in a blue golfer and cap, and prettily flushed by the keen air to the colour of a pink shell, her quick eyes took in every detail of Jane's attire before she was introduced, and her mother guessed a suppressed twinkle in her smile. Mrs. Oliver hoped Daphne was going to be polite to these visitors. She was afraid Daphne was in a rather perverse mood towards Eddy's friends. Denison, of course, she frankly disliked, and did not make much secret of it. He was conceited, plain, his hair untidy, his collar low, and his manners supercilious. Denison was well equipped for taking care of himself; those who came to blows with him rarely came off best. He behaved very well at tea, knowing, as Eddy had said, that it was a Deanery. But he was annoying once. Someone had given Mrs. Oliver at Christmas a certain book, containing many beautiful and tranquil thoughts about this world, its inhabitants, its origin, and its goal, by a writer who had produced, and would, no doubt, continue to produce, very many such books. Many people read this writer constantly, and got help therefrom, and often wrote and told him so; others did not read him at all, not finding life long enough; others, again, read him sometimes in an idle moment, to get a little diversion. Of these last was Arnold Denison. When he put his tea-cup down on the table at his side, his eye chanced on the beautiful book lying thereon, and he laughed a little.

"Which one is that? Oh, *Garden Paths*. That's the last but two, isn't it." He picked it up and turned the leaves, and chuckled at a certain passage, which he proceeded to read aloud. It had, unfortunately, or was intended to have, a philosophical and more or less religious bearing (the writer was a vague but zealous seeker after truth); also, more unfortunately still, the Dean and his wife knew the author; in fact, he had stayed with them often. Eddy would have warned Arnold of that had he had time, but it was too late. He could only now say, "I call that very interesting, and jolly well put."

The Dean said, genially, but with acerbity, "Ah, you mustn't make game of Phil Underwood here, you know; he's a *persona grata* with us. A dear fellow. And not in the least spoilt by all his tremendous success. As candid and unaffected as he was when we were at Cambridge together, five and thirty years ago. And look at all he's done since then. He's walked straight into the heart of the reading public—the more thoughtful and discriminating part of it, that is, for of course he's not any man's fare—not showy enough; he's not one of your smart paradox-and-epigram-mongers. He leads one by very quiet and delightful paths, right out of the noisy world. A great rest and refreshment for busy men and women; we want more like him in this hurrying age, when most people's chief object seems to be to see how much they can get done in how short a time."

"*He's* fairly good at that, you know," suggested Arnold, innocently turning to the title-page of the last but two, to find its date.

Mrs. Oliver said, gently, but a little distantly, "I always feel it rather a pity to make fun of a writer who has helped so many people so very greatly as Philip Underwood has," which was damping and final, and the sort of unfair thing, Arnold felt, that shouldn't be said in conversation. That is the worst of people who aren't clever; they suddenly turn on you and score heavily, and you can't get even. So he said, bored, "Shall I come down with you to meet Eileen, Eddy?" and Daphne thought he had rotten manners and had cheeked her parents. He and Eddy went out together, to meet Eileen.

It was characteristic of Jane that she had given no contribution to this conversation, never having read any Philip Underwood, and only very vaguely and remotely having heard of him. Jane was marvellously good at concerning herself only with the first-rate; hence she never sneered at the second or third-rate, for it had no existence for her. She was not one of those artists who mock at the Royal Academy; she never saw most of the pictures there exhibited, but only the few she wished to see, and went on purpose to see. Neither did she jeer at even our most popular writers of fiction, nor at Philip Underwood. Jane was very cloistered, very chaste. Whatsoever things were lovely, she thought on these things, and on no others. At the present moment she was thinking of the Deanery hall, how beautifully it was shaped, and how good was the curve of the oak stairs up from it, and how pleasing and worth drawing Daphne's long, irregular, delicately-tinted face, with the humorous, one-sided, half-reluctant smile, and the golden waves of hair beneath the blue cap. She wondered if Daphne would let her make a sketch. She would draw her as some little vagabond, amused, sullen, elfish, half-tamed, wholly spoilt, preferably in rags, and bare-limbed— Jane's fingers itched to be at work on her.

Rather a silent girl, Mrs. Oliver decided, and said, "You must go over the Cathedral to-morrow."

Jane agreed that she must, and Daphne hoped that Eddy would do that business. For her, she was sick of showing people the Cathedral, and conducting them to the Early English door and the Norman arches, and the something else Lady-chapel, and all the rest of the tiresome things the guide-book superfluously put it into people's heads to inquire after. One took aunts round.... But whenever Daphne could, she left it to the Dean, who enjoyed it, and had, of course, very much more to say about it, knowing not only every detail of its architecture and history, but every detail of its needed repairs and pinnings-up, and general improvements, and how long they would take to do, and how little money was at present forthcoming to do them with. The Dean was as keen on his Cathedral as on revision. Mrs. Oliver had the knowledge of it customary with people of culture who live near cathedrals, and Eddy that and something more, added by a great affection. The Cathedral for him had a glamour and glory.

The Dean began to tell Jane about it.

"You are an artist, Eddy tells us," he said, presently; "well, I think certain bits of our Cathedral must be an inspiration to any artist. Do you know Wilson Gavin's studies of details of Ely? Very exquisite and delicate work."

Jane thought so too.

"Poor Gavin," the Dean added, more gravely; "we used to see something of him when he came down to Ely, five or six years ago. It's an extraordinary thing that he could do work like that, so marvellously pure and delicate, and full, apparently of such reverent love of beauty—and at the same time lead the life he has led since, and I suppose is leading now."

Jane looked puzzled.

The Dean said, "Ah, of course, you don't know him. But one hears sad stories...."

"I know Mr. Gavin a little," said Jane. "I always like him very much."

The Dean thought her either not nearly particular enough, or too ignorant to be credible. She obviously either had never heard, had quite forgotten, or didn't mind, the sad stories. He hoped for the best, and dropped the subject. He couldn't well say straight out, before Miss Dawn and Daphne, that he had heard that Mr. Gavin had eloped with someone else's wife.

It was perhaps for the best that Eddy and Arnold and Eileen arrived at this moment.

At a glance the Olivers saw that Mrs. Le Moine was different from Miss Dawn. She was charmingly dressed. She had a blue travelling-coat, grey furs, deep blue eyes under black brows, and an engaging smile. Certainly "rather beautiful," as Eddy had said to Daphne, and of a charm that they all felt, but especially the Dean.

Mrs. Oliver, catching Eddy's eye as he introduced her, saw that he was proud of this one among his visitors. She knew the look, radiant, half shy, the look of a nice child introducing an admired school friend to his people, sure they will get on, thinking how jolly for both of them to know each other. The less nice child has a different look, mistrustful, nervous, anxious, lest his people should disgrace themselves....

Mrs. Oliver gave Mrs. Le Moine tea. They all talked. Eileen had brought in with her a periodical she had been reading in the train, which had in it a poem by Billy Raymond. Arnold picked it up and read it, and said he was sorry about it. Eddy then read it and said, "I rather like it. Don't you, Eileen? It's very much Billy in a certain mood, of course."

Arnold said it was Billy reacting with such violence against Masefield—a very sensible procedure within limits—that he had all but landed himself in the impressionist preciosity of the early Edwardians.

Eileen said, "It's Billy when he's been lunching with Cecil. He's often taken like that then."

The Dean said, "And who's Cecil?"

Eileen said, "My husband," and the Dean and Mrs. Oliver weren't sure if, given one was living apart from one's husband, it was quite nice to mention him casually at tea like that; more particularly when he had just written a censored play.

The Dean, in order not to pursue the subject of Mr. Le Moine, held out his hand for the *Blue Review*, and perused Billy's production, which was called "The Mussel Picker."

He laid it down presently and said, "I can't say I gather any very coherent thought from it."

Arnold said, "Quite. Billy hadn't any just then. That is wholly obvious. Billy sometimes has, but occasionally hasn't, you know. Billy is at times, though by no means always, a shallow young man."

"Shallow young men produce a good deal of our modern poetry, it seems to me from my slight acquaintance with it," said the Dean. "One misses the thought in it that made the Victorian giants so fine."

As a good many of the shallow young producers of our modern poetry were more or less intimately known to his three guests, Arnold suspected the Dean of trying to get back on him for his aspersions on Philip Underwood. He with difficulty restrained himself from saying, gently but aloofly, *a la* Mrs. Oliver, "I always think it rather a pity to criticize writers who have helped so many people so very greatly as our Georgian poets have," and said instead, "But the point about this thing of Billy's is that it's not modern in the least. It breathes of fifteen years back—the time when people painted in words, and were all for atmosphere. Surely whatever you say about the best modern people, you can't deny they're full of thought—so full that sometimes they forget the sound and everything else. Of course you mayn't *like* the thought, that's quite another thing; but you can't miss it; it fairly jumps out at you.... Did you read John Henderson's thing in this month's *English Review*?"

This was one of the periodicals not taken in at the Deanery, so the Dean hadn't read it. Nor did he want to enter into an argument on modern poetry, with which he was less familiar than with the Victorian giants.

Arnold, talking too much, as he often did when not talking too little, said across the room to Daphne, "What do *you* think of John Henderson, Miss Oliver?"

It amused him to provoke her, because she was a match for him in rudeness, and drew him too by her attractive face and abrupt speech. She wasn't dull, though she might care nothing for John Henderson or any other poet, and looked on and yawned when she was bored.

"Never thought about him at all," she said now. "Who is he?" though she knew quite well.

Arnold proceeded to tell her, with elaboration and diffuseness.

"I can lend you his works, if you'd like," he added.

She said, "No, thanks," and Mrs. Oliver said, "I'm afraid we don't find very much time for casual reading here, Mr. Denison," meaning that she didn't think John Henderson proper for Daphne, because he was sometimes coarse, and she suspected him of being free-thinking, though as a matter of fact he was ardently and even passionately religious, in a way hardly fit for deaneries.

"*I* don't read John's things, you know, Arnold," put in Jane. "I don't like them much. He said I'd better not try, as he didn't suppose I should ever get to like them better."

"That's John all over," said Eileen. "He's so nice and untouchy. Fancy Cecil saying that—except in bitter sarcasm. John's a dear, so he is. Though he read worse last Tuesday at the Bookshop than I've ever heard anyone. You'd think he had a plum in his mouth."

Obviously these young people were much interested in poets and poetry. So Mrs. Oliver said, "On the last night of the year, the Dean usually reads us some poetry, just before the clock strikes. Very often he reads Tennyson's 'Ring out, wild bells.' It is an old family custom of ours," she added, and they all said what a good one, and how nice it would be. Then Mrs. Oliver told them that they weren't to dress for dinner, because there was evensong afterwards in the Cathedral, on account of New Year's Eve.

"But you needn't go unless you want to," Daphne added, enviously. Herself she had to go, whether she wanted to or not.

"I'd like to," Eileen said.

"It's a way of seeing the Cathedral, of course," said Eddy. "It's rather beautiful by candlelight."

So they all settled to go, even Arnold, who thought that of all the ways of seeing the Cathedral, that was the least good. However, he went, and when they came back they settled down for a festive night, playing coon-can and the pianola, and preparing punch, till half-past eleven, when the Dean came in from his study with Tennyson, and read "Ring out, wild bells." At five minutes to twelve they began listening for the clock to strike, and when it had struck and been duly counted, they drank each other a happy new year in punch, except Jane, who disliked whisky too much to drink it, and had lemonade instead. In short, they formed one of the many happy homes of England who were seeing the old year out in the same cheerful and friendly manner. Having done so, they went to bed.

"Eddy in the home is entirely a dear," Eileen said to Jane, lingering a moment by Jane's fire before she went to her own. "He's such—such a good boy, isn't he?" She leant on the words, with a touch of tenderness and raillery. Then she added, "But, Jane, we shall have his parents shocked before we go. It would be easily done. In fact, I'm not sure we've not done it already, a little. Arnold is so reckless, and you so ingenuous, and myself so ambiguous in position. I've a fear they think us a little unconventional, no less, and are nervous about our being too much with the pretty little sulky sister. But I expect she'll see to that herself; we bore her, do you know. And Arnold insists on annoying her, which is tiresome of him."

"She looks rather sweet when she's cross," said Jane, regarding the matter professionally. "I should like to draw her then. Eddy's people are very nice, only not very peaceful, somehow, do you think? I don't know why, but one feels a little tired after talking much to them; perhaps it's because of what you say, that they might easily be shocked; and besides, one doesn't quite always understand what they say. At least, I don't; but I'm stupid at understanding people, I know."

Jane sighed a little, and let her wavy brown hair fall in two smooth strands on either side of her small pale face. The Deanery was full of strange standards and codes and values, alien and unintelligible. Jane didn't know even what they were, though Eileen and Arnold, living in a less rarefied, more in-the-world atmosphere, could have enlightened her about many of them. It mattered in the Deanery what one's father was; quite kindly but quite definitely note was taken of that; Mrs. Oliver valued birth and breeding, though she was not snobbish, and was quite prepared to be kind and friendly to those without it. Also it mattered how one dressed; whether one had on usual, tidy, and sufficiently expensive clothes; whether, in fact, one displayed good taste in the matter, and was neither cheap nor showy, but suitable to the hour and occasion. These things do matter, it is very certain. Also it mattered that one should be able to find one's way about a Church of England Prayer Book during a service, a task at which Jane and Eileen were both incompetent. Jane had not been brought up to follow services in a book, only to sit in college ante-chapels and listen to anthems; and Eileen, reared by an increasingly anti-clerical father, had drifted fitfully in and out of Roman Catholic churches as a child in Ireland, and had since never attended any. Consequently they had helplessly fumbled with their books at evening service. Arnold, who had received the sound Church education (sublimely independent of personal fancies as to belief or disbelief) of our English male youth at school and college, knew all about it, and showed Jane how to find the Psalms, while Eddy performed the same office for Eileen. Daphne looked on with cynical amusement, and Mrs. Oliver with genuine shocked feeling.

"Anyhow," said Daphne to her mother afterwards, "I should think they'll agree with father that it wants revising."

Next day they all went tobogganing, and met the Bellairs family. Eddy threw Molly and Eileen together, because he wanted them to make friends, which Daphne resented, because she wanted to talk to Molly herself, and Eileen made her feel shy. When she was alone with Molly she said, "What do you think of Eddy's friends?"

"Mrs. Le Moine is very charming," said Molly, an appreciative person. "She's so awfully pretty, isn't she? And Miss Dawn seems rather sweet, and Mr. Denison's very clever, I should think."

Daphne sniffed. "He thinks so, too. I expect they all think they're jolly clever. But those two"—she indicated Eileen and Jane—"can't find their places in their Prayer Books without being shown. I don't call that very clever."

"How funny," said Molly.

Acrimony was added to Daphne's view of Eileen by Claude Bellairs, who looked at her as if he admired her. Claude as a rule looked at Daphne herself like that; Daphne didn't want him to, thinking it silly, but it was rather much to have his admiration transferred to this Mrs. Le Moine. Certainly anyone might have admired Eileen; Daphne grudgingly admitted that, as she watched her. Eileen's manner of accepting attentions was as lazy and casual as Daphne's own, and considerably less provocative; she couldn't be said to encourage them. Only there was a charm about her, a drawing-power....

"*I* don't think it's nice, a married person letting men hang round her," said Daphne, who was rather vulgar.

Molly, who was refined, coloured all over her round, sensitive face.

"Daffy! How can you? Of course it's all right."

"Well, Claude would be flirting in no time if she let him."

"But of course she wouldn't. How could she?" Molly was dreadfully shocked.

Daphne gave her cynical, one-sided smile. "Easily, I should think. Only probably she doesn't think him worth while."

"Daffy, I think it's horrible to talk like that. I do wish you wouldn't."

"All right. Come on and have a go down the hill, then."

The Bellairs' came to dinner that evening. Molly was a little subdued, and with her usual flow of childish high spirits not quite so spontaneous as usual. She sat between Eddy and the Dean, and was rather quiet with both of them. The Dean took in Eileen, and on her other side was Nevill Bellairs, who, having deduced in the afternoon that she was partly Irish, very naturally mentioned the Home Rule Bill, which he had been spending last session largely in voting against. Being Irish, Mrs. Le Moine presumably felt strongly on this subject, which he introduced with the complacency of one who had been fighting in her cause. She listened to him with her half railing, inscrutable smile, until Eddy said across the table, "Mrs. Le Moine's a Home Ruler, Nevill; look out," and Nevill stopped abruptly in full flow and said, "You're not!" and pretended not to mind, and to be only disconcerted for himself, but was really indignant with her for being such a thing, and a little with Eddy for not having warned him. It dried up his best conversation, as one couldn't talk politics to a Home Ruler. He wondered was she a Papist, too. So he talked about hunting in Ireland, and found she knew nothing of hunting there or indeed anywhere. Then he tried London, but found that the London she knew was different from his, except externally, and you can't talk for ever about streets and buildings, especially if you do not frequent the same eating-places. From different eating-places the world is viewed from different angles; few things are a more significant test of a person's point of view.

Meanwhile the Dean was telling Jane about places of interest, such as Roman camps, in the neighbourhood. The Dean, like many deans, talked rather well. He thought Jane prettily attentive, and more educated than most young women, and that it was a pity she wore such an old-fashioned dress. He did not say so, but asked her if she had designed it from Carpaccio's St. Ursula, and she said no, from an angel playing the timbrel by Jacopo Bellini in the Accademia. So after that they talked about Venice, and he said he must show her his photographs of it after dinner. "It must be a wonderful place for an artist," he told her, and she agreed, and then they compared notes and found that he had stayed at the Hotel Europa, and had had a lovely view of the Giudecca and Santa Maria Maggiore from the windows ("most exquisite on a grey day"), and she had stayed in the flat of an artist friend, looking on to the Rio delle Beccarie, which is a *rio* of the poor. Like Eileen and Nevill, they had eaten in different places; but, unlike London, Venice is a coherent whole, not rings within rings, so they could talk, albeit with reservations and a few cross purposes. The Dean liked talking about pictures, and Torcello, and Ruskin, and St. Mark's, and the other things one talks about when one has been to Venice. Perhaps too he even wanted a little to hear her talk about them, feeling interested in the impressions of an artist. Jane was rather disappointingly simple and practical on these subjects; artists, like other experts, are apt to leave rhapsodies to the layman, and tacitly assume admiration of the beauty that is dilated on by the unprofessional. They are baffling people; the Dean remembered that about poor Wilson Gavin.

While he thus held Jane's attention, Eddy talked to Molly about skating, a subject in which both were keenly interested, Daphne sparred with Claude, and Arnold entertained Mrs. Oliver, whom he found a little *difficile* and rather the *grande dame*. Frankly, Mrs. Oliver did not like Arnold, and he saw through her courtesy as easily as through Daphne's rudeness. She thought him conceited (which he was), irreverent (which he was also), worldly (which he was not), and a bad influence over Eddy (and whether he was that depended on what you meant by "bad").

On the whole it was rather an uncomfortable dinner, as dinners go. There was a sense of misfit about it. There were just enough people at cross-purposes to give a feeling of strain, a feeling felt most strongly by Eddy, who had perceptions, and particularly wanted the evening to be a success. Even Molly and he had somehow come up against something, a rock below the cheerful, friendly stream of their intercourse, that pulled him up, though he didn't understand what it was. There was a spiritual clash somewhere, between nearly every two of them. Between him and Molly it was all her doing; he had never felt friendlier; it was she who had put up a queer, vague wall. He could not see into her mind, so he didn't bother about it much but went on being cheerful and friendly.

They were all happier after dinner, when playing the pianola in the hall and dancing to it.

But on the whole the evening was only a moderate success.

The Bellairs' told their parents afterwards that they didn't much care about the friends Eddy had staying.

"*I* believe they're stuck up," said Dick (the Guards), who hadn't been at dinner, but had met them tobogganing. "That man Denison's for ever trying to be clever. I can't stand that; it's such beastly bad form. Don't think he succeeds, either, if you ask me. I can't see it's particularly clever to be always sneering at things one knows nothing about. Can't think why Eddy likes him. He's not a bit keen on the things Eddy's keen on—hunting, or shooting, or games, or soldiering."

"There are lots like him at Oxford," said Claude. "I know the type. Balliol's full of it. Awfully unwholesome, and a great bore to meet. They write things, and admire each other's. I suppose it's the same at Cambridge. Only I should have thought Eddy would have kept out of the way of it."

Claude had been disgusted by what he considered Arnold's rudeness to Daphne. "I thought Mrs. Le Moine seemed rather nice, though," he added.

"Well, I must say," Nevill said, "she was a little too much for me. English Home Rulers are bad enough, but at least they know nothing about it and are usually merely silly; but Irish ones are more than I can stand. Eddy told me afterwards that her father was that fellow Conolly, who runs the *Hibernian*—the most disloyal rag that ever throve in a Dublin gutter. It does more harm than any other paper in Ireland, I believe. What can you expect of his daughter, let alone a woman married to a disreputable play-writer, and not even living with him? I rather wonder Mrs. Oliver likes to have her in the house with Daphne."

"Miss—what d'you call her—Morning—seemed harmless, but a little off it," said Dick. "She doesn't talk too much, anyhow, like Denison. Queer things she wears, though. And she doesn't know much about London, for a person who lives there, I must say. Doesn't seem to have seen any of the plays. Rather vague, somehow, she struck me as being."

Claude groaned. "So would her father if you met him. A fearful old dreamer. I coach with him in Political Science. He's considered a great swell; I was told I was lucky to get him; but I can't make head or tail of him or his books. His daughter has just his absent eye."

"Poor things," said Mrs. Bellairs, sleepily. "And poor Mrs. Oliver and the Dean. I wonder how long these unfortunate people are staying, and if we ought to ask them over one day?"

But none of her children appeared to think they ought. Even Molly, always loyal, always hospitable, always generous, didn't think so. For stronger in Molly's child-like soul than even her loyalty and her hospitality, and her generosity, was her moral sense, and this was questioning, shamefacedly, reluctantly, whether these friends of Eddy's were really "good."

So they didn't ask them over.

CHAPTER VIII.

THE VISITORS GO.

NEXT morning Eileen got a letter. She read it before breakfast, turned rather paler, and looked up at Eddy as if she was trying to bring her mind back from a great distance. In her eyes was fear, and that look of brooding, soft pity that he had learnt to associate with one only of Eileen's friends.

She said, "Hugh's ill," frowning at him absently, and added, "I must go to him, this morning. He's alone," and Eddy remembered a paragraph he had seen in the *Morning Post* about Lady Dorothy Datcherd and the Riviera. Lady Dorothy never stayed with Datcherd when he was ill. Periodically his lungs got much worse, and he had to lie up, and he hated that.

"Does he write himself?" Arnold asked. He was fond of Hugh Datcherd.

"Yes—oh, he doesn't say he's ill, he never will, but I know it by his writing—I must go by the next train, I'm afraid"; she remembered to turn to Mrs. Oliver and speak apologetically. "I'm very sorry to be so sudden."

"We are so sorry for the cause," said Mrs. Oliver, courteously. "Is it your brother?" (Surely it wouldn't be her husband, in the circumstances?)

"It is not," said Eileen, still abstracted. "It's a friend. He's alone, and consumptive, and if he's not looked after he destroys himself doing quite mad things. His wife's gone away."

Mrs. Oliver became a shade less sympathetic. It was a pity it was not a brother, which would have been more natural. However, Mrs. Le Moine was, of course, a married woman, though under curious circumstances. She began to discuss trains, and the pony-carriage, and sandwiches.

Eddy explained afterwards while Eileen was upstairs.

"It's Hugh Datcherd, a great friend of hers; poor chap, his lungs are frightfully gone, I'm afraid. He's an extraordinarily interesting and capable man; runs an enormous settlement in North-East London, and has any number of different social schemes all over the place. He edits *Further*—do you ever see it, father?"

"*Further?* Yes, it's been brought to my notice once or twice. It goes a good way 'further' than even our poor heretical deans, doesn't it?"

It went in a quite different direction, Eddy thought. Our heretical deans do not always go very far along the road which leads to social betterment and slum-destroying; they are often too busy improving theology to have much time to improve houses.

"An able man, I daresay," said the Dean. "Like all the Datcherds. Most of them have been Parliamentary, of course. Two Datcherds were at Cambridge with me—Roger and Stephen; this man's uncles, I suppose; his father would be before my time. They were both very brilliant fellows, and fine speakers at the Union, and have become capable Parliamentary speakers now. A family of hereditary Whigs; but this man's the only out and out Radical, I should say. A pity he's so bitter against Christianity."

"He's not bitter," said Eddy. "He's very gentle. Only he disbelieves in it as a means of progress."

"Surely," said Mrs. Oliver, "he married one of Lord Ulverstone's daughters—Dorothy, wasn't it." (Lord Ulverstone and Mrs. Oliver's family were both of Westmorland, where there is strong clannish feeling.)

"He and Dorothy don't seem to be hitting it off, do they," put in Daphne, and her mother said, "Daphne, dear," and changed the subject. Daphne ought not, by good rights, to have heard that about Hugh Datcherd being ill and alone, and Mrs. Le Moine going to him.

"She's a trying woman, I fancy," said Eddy, who did not mean to be tactless, but had been absorbed in his own thoughts and had got left behind when his mother started a new subject. "Hard, and selfish, and extravagant, and thinks of nothing but amusing herself, and doesn't care a hang for any of Datcherd's schemes, or for Datcherd himself, for that matter. She just goes off and leaves him to be ill by himself. He nearly died last year; he was awfully cut up, too, about their little girl dying—she was the only child, and Datcherd was absolutely devoted to her, and I believe her mother neglected her when she was ill, just as she does Datcherd."

"These stories get exaggerated, of course," said Mrs. Oliver, because Lady Dorothy was one of the Westmorland Ulverstones, because Daphne was listening, and because she suspected the source of the stories to be Eileen Le Moine.

"Oh, I've no doubt there's her side of it, too, if one knew it," admitted Eddy, ready, as usual, to see everyone's point of view. "It would be a frightful bore being married to a man who was interested in all the things you hated most, and gave his whole time and money and energy to them. But anyhow, you see why his friends, and particularly Eileen, who's his greatest friend, feel responsible for him."

"A very sad state of things," said Mrs. Oliver.

"Anyhow," said Daphne, "here's the pony-trap."

Eileen came downstairs, hand-in-hand with Jane, and said goodbye to the Dean, and Mrs. Oliver, and Daphne, and "Thank you so much for having me," and drove off with Eddy and Jane, still with that look of troubled wistfulness in her face.

She smiled faintly at Eddy from the train.

"I'm sorry, Eddy. It's a shame I have to go," but her thoughts were not for him, as he knew.

Outside the station they met Arnold, and he and Jane walked off together to see something in the Cathedral, while Eddy drove home.

Jane gave a little pitiful sigh. "Poor dears," she murmured.

"H'm?" questioned Arnold, who was interested in the streets.

"Poor Eileen," Jane amplified; "poor Hugh."

"Oh, quite," Arnold nodded. But, feeling more interested in ideas than in people, he talked about Welchester.

"The stuffiness of the place!" he commented, with energy of abuse. "The stodginess. The canons and their wives. The—the enlightened culture of the Deanery. The propriety. The correctness. The intelligence. The cathedralism. The good breeding. How can Eddy bear it, Jane? Why doesn't he kick someone or something over and run?"

"Eddy likes it," said Jane. "He's very fond of it. After all, it is rather exquisite; look——"

They had stopped at the end of Church Street, and looked along its narrow length to the square that opened out before the splendid West Front. Arnold screwed up his eyes at it, appreciatively.

"*That's* all right. It's the people I'm thinking of."

"But you know, Arnold, Eddy's not exclusive like most people, like you and me, and—and Mrs. Oliver, and those nice Bellairs'. He likes everyone and everything. Things are delightful to him merely because they exist."

Arnold groaned. "Whitman said that before you, the brute. If I thought Eddy had anything in common with Walt, our friendship would end forthwith."

"He has nothing whatever," Jane reassured him, placidly. "Whitman hated all sorts of things. Whitman's more like you; he'd have hated Welchester."

"Yes, I'm afraid that's true. The cleanliness, the cant, the smug faces of men and women in the street, the worshippers in cathedrals, the keepers of Sabbaths, the respectable and the well-to-do, the Sunday hats and black coats of the men, the panaches and tight skirts of the women, the tea-fights, the well-read deans and their lady-like wives—what have I to do with these or these with me? All, all of them I loathe; away with them, I will not have them near me any more. *Allons, camerado*, I will take to the open road beneath the stars.... What a pity he would have said that; but I can't alter my opinion, even for him.... How at home dear old Phil Underwood would be here, wouldn't he. How he must enjoy his visits to the Deanery, where he's a *persona grata*. And how he must bore the young sister. *She's* all right, you know, Jane. I rather like her. And she hates me. She's quite genuine, and free from cant; just as worldly as they make 'em, and never pretends to be anything else. Besides, she's all alive; rather like a young wild animal. It's queer she and Eddy being brother and sister, she so decided and fixed in all her opinions and rejections, and he so impressionable. Oh, another thing—I have an unhappy feeling that Eddy is going, eventually, to marry that little yellow-eyed girl—Miss Bellairs. Somehow I feel it."

Jane said, "Nonsense," and laughed. "She's not a bit the sort."

"Of course she's not. But to Eddy, as you observed, all sorts are acceptable. She's one sort, you'll admit. And one he's attached to—wind and weather and jolly adventures and old companionship, she stands for to him. Not a subtle appeal, but still, an appeal. They're fond of each other, and it will turn to that, you'll see. Eddy never says, "That's not the sort of thing, or the sort of person, for me." Because they all are. Look at the way he swallowed those parsons down in his slum. Swallowed them—why, he loves them. Look at the way he accepts Welchester, stodginess and all, and likes it. He was the same at Cambridge; nothing was outside the range for him; he never drew the line. I'm really not particular"—Jane laughed at him again—"but I tell you he consorted sometimes with the most utterly utter, and didn't seem to mind. Kept very bad company indeed on occasion; company the Dean wouldn't at all have approved of, I'm sure. Many times I've had to step in and try in vain to haul him by force out of some select set. Nuts, smugs, pious men, betting *roués*, beefy hulks—all were grist to his mill. And still it's the same. Miss Bellairs, no doubt, is a very nice girl, quite genuine and natural, and rather like a jolly kitten, which is always attractive. But she's rigid within; she won't mix with the people Eddy will want to mix with. She's not comprehensive. She wouldn't like us much, for instance; she'd think us rather queer and shady beings, not what she's used to or understands. We should worry and puzzle her. She's gay and sweet and unselfish, and good, sweet maid, and lets who will be clever. Lets them, but doesn't want to have much to do with them. She'll shut us all out, and try to shut Eddy in with her. She won't succeed, because he'll go on wanting a little bit of all there is, and so they'll both be miserable. Her share of the world, you see—all the share she asks for—is homogeneous; his is heterogeneous, a sort of gypsy stew with everything in it. You may say that he's greedy for mixed fare, while she has a simple and fastidious appetite. There are the materials for another unhappy marriage ready provided."

Jane was looking at the Prior's Door with her head on one side. She smiled at it peacefully.

"Really, Arnold——"

"Oh, I know. You're going to say, what reason have I for supposing that Eddy has ever thought of this young girl in that way, as they say in fiction. I don't say he has yet. But he will. Propinquity will do it, and common tastes, and old affection. You'll see, Jane. I'm not often wrong about these unfortunate affairs. I dislike them so much that it gives me an instinct."

Jane shook her head. "I think Welchester is affecting you for bad, Arnold. That, you know, is what the people who annoy you so much here would do, I expect—look at all affection and friendship like that."

"That's true." Arnold looked at her in surprise. "But I shouldn't have expected you to know it. You are improving in perspicacity, Jane; it's the first time I have known you aware of the vulgarity about you."

Jane looked a little proud of herself, as she only did when she had displayed a piece of worldly knowledge. She did not say that she had obtained her knowledge from Mrs. Oliver and the Dean, who, watching Eddy and Eileen, had too obviously done so with troubled eyes, so that she longed to comfort them with explanations they would never understand.

It was certain that they were relieved that Eileen had gone, though the reason of her going had placed her in a more dubious light. Also, she forgot, unfortunately, to write her bread and butter letter. "I suppose she can't spare the time from Hugh," said Daphne. But she wrote to Jane, telling her that Hugh was laid up with hemorrhage, and had been ordered to go away directly he was fit. "They say Davos, but he won't. I don't know where it will be." Jane, whose worldly shrewdness after all had narrow limits, repeated this to Eddy in his mother's presence.

"Has his wife got back yet?" Mrs. Oliver inquired gravely, and Jane shook her head. "Oh no. She won't. She's spending the winter on the Riviera."

"I should think Mr. Datcherd too had better spend the winter on the Riviera," suggested Mrs. Oliver.

"Isn't it rather bad for consumption?" said Eddy, shirking issues other than hygienic.

"I believe," said Jane, not shirking them, "his wife isn't coming back to him at all again. She's tired of him, I'm afraid. I daresay it's a good thing; she is very irritating and difficult."

Mrs. Oliver changed the subject. These seemed to her what women in her district would have called strange goings on. She commented on them to the Dean, who, more tolerant, said, "One must allow some licence to genius, I suppose." Perhaps: but the question was, how much. Genius might alter manners—(for the worse, Mrs. Oliver thought)—but it shouldn't be allowed to alter morals.

"Anyhow," said Mrs. Oliver, "I am rather troubled that Eddy should be so intimate with these people."

"Eddy is a steady-headed boy," said the Dean. "He knows where to draw the line." Which is what parents often think of their children, with how little warrant! Drawing the line was precisely the art which, Arnold complained, Eddy had not learnt at all.

Jane and Arnold stayed three days more at the Deanery. Jane drew details of the Cathedral and studies of Daphne. The Dean thought, as he had often thought before, that artists were interesting, child-like, but rather baffling people, incredibly innocent, or else incredibly apt to accept moral evil with indifference; also that, though, he feared, quite outside the Church, and what he considered to be pagan in outlook, she displayed, like poor Wilson Gavin, a very delicate appreciation of ecclesiastical architecture and religious art.

Mrs. Oliver thought her more unconventional and lacking in knowledge of the world than any girl had a right to be.

Daphne and the Bellairs family thought her a harmless crank, who took off her hat in the road.

The Bellairs' supposed she must Want a Vote, till she announced her indifference on that subject, which disgusted Daphne, an ardent and potentially militant suffragist, and disappointed her mother, a calm but earnest member of the National Union for Women's Suffrage, who went to meetings Daphne was not allowed at. Jane—perhaps it was because of the queer sexlessness which was part of her charm, perhaps because of being an artist, and other-worldly—seemed to care little for women's rights or women's wrongs. Mrs. Oliver noted that her social conscience was unawakened, and thought her selfish. Artists were perhaps like that—wrapped up in their own joy of the lovely world, so that they never turned and looked into the shadows. Eddy, a keen suffragist himself, said it was because Jane had never lived among the very poor.

"She should use her power of vision," said the Dean. "She's got plenty."

"She's one-windowed," Eddy explained. "She only looks out on to the beautiful things; she has a blank wall between her and the ugly."

"In plain words, a selfish young woman," said Mrs. Oliver, but to herself.

So much for Jane. Arnold was more severely condemned. The more they all saw of him, the less they liked him, and the more supercilious he grew. Even at times he stopped remembering it was a Deanery, though he really tried to do this. But the atmosphere did annoy him.

"Mr. Denison has really very unfortunate ways of expressing himself at times," said Mrs. Oliver, who had too, Arnold thought.

"Oh, he means well," said Eddy apologetic. "You mustn't mind him. He's got corns, and if anyone steps on them he turns nasty. He's always like that."

"In fact, a conceited pig," said Daphne, not to herself.

Personally Daphne thought the best of the three was Mrs. Le Moine, who anyhow dressed well and could dance, though her habits might be queer. Better queer habits than queer clothes, any day, thought Daphne, innately a pagan, with the artist's eye and the materialist's soul.

Anyhow, Jane and Arnold departed on Monday. From the point of view of Mrs. Oliver and the Dean, it might have been better had it been Saturday, as their ideas of how to spend Sunday had been revealed as unfitting a Deanery. The Olivers were not in the least sabbatarian, they were much too wide-minded for that, but they thought their visitors should go to church once during the day. Perhaps Jane had been discouraged by her experiences with the Prayer Book on New Year's Eve. Perhaps it never occurred to her to go. Anyhow in the morning she stayed at home and drew, and in the evening wandered into the Cathedral during the collects, stayed for the anthem, and wandered out, peaceful and content, with no suspicion of having done the wrong or unusual thing. Arnold lay in the hall all the morning and smoked and read *The New Machiavelli*, which was one of the books not liked at the Deanery. (Arnold, by the way, didn't like it much either, but dipped in and out of it, grunting when bored.) In consequence (not in consequence of *The New Machiavelli*, which she would have found dull, but of being obliged herself to go to church), Daphne was cross and envious, the Dean and his wife slightly disapproving, and Eddy sorry about the misunderstanding.

On the whole, the visit had not been the success Eddy had wished for. He felt that. In spite of some honest endeavour on both sides, the hosts and guests had not fitted into each other.

Coming back into Welchester from a walk, and seeing its streets full of peace and blue winter twilight and starred with yellow lamps, Eddy thought it queer that there should be disharmonies in such a place. It had peace, and a wistful, ordered beauty, and dignity, and grace....

They were singing in the Cathedral, and lights glowed redly through the stained windows. Strangely the place transcended all factions, all barriers, proving them illusions in the still light of the Real. Eddy, beneath all his ineffectualities, his futilities of life and thought, had a very keen sense of unity, of the coherence of all beauty and good; in a sense he did really transcend the barriers recognised by less shallow people. With a welcoming leap his heart went out to embrace all beauty, all truth. Surely one could afford to miss no aspect of it through blindness. Open-eyed he looked into the blue night of lamps and shadows and men and women, and beyond it to the stars and the sickle of the moon, and all of it crowded into his vision, and he caught his breath a little and smiled, because it was so good and so much.

When he got home he saw his mother sitting in the hall, reading the *Times*. Moved by love and liking, he put his arm round her shoulders and bent over her and kissed her. The grace, the breeding, the culture—she was surely part of it all, and should make, like the Cathedral, for harmony. Arnold had found Mrs. Oliver commonplace. Eddy found her admirable. Jane had not found her at all. There was the difference between them. Undoubtedly Eddy's, whether the most truthful way or not, was the least wasteful.

CHAPTER IX.

THE CLUB.

SOON after Eddy's return to London, Eileen Le Moine wrote and asked him to meet her at lunch at a restaurant in Old Compton Street. It was a rather more select restaurant than they and their friends usually frequented in Soho, so Eddy divined that she wanted to speak to him alone and uninterrupted. She arrived late, as always, and pale, and a little abstracted, as if she were tired in mind or body, but her smile flashed out at him, radiant and kind. Direct and to the point, as usual, she began at once, as they began to eat risotto, "I wonder would you do something for Hugh?"

Eddy said, "I expect so," and added, "I hope he's much better?"

"He is not," she told him. "The doctor says he must go away—out of England—for quite a month, and have no bother or work at all. It's partly nerves, you see, and over-work. Someone will have to go with him, to look after him, but they've not settled who yet. He'll probably go to Greece, and walk about.... Anyhow he's to be away somewhere.... And he's been destroying himself with worry because he must leave his work—the settlement and everything—and he's afraid it will go to pieces. You know he has the Club House open every evening for the boys and young men, and goes down there himself several nights a week. What we thought was that perhaps you wouldn't mind taking charge, being generally responsible, in fact. There are several helpers, of course, but Hugh wants someone to see after it and get people to give lectures and keep the thing going. We thought you'd perhaps have the time, and we knew you had the experience and could do it. It's very important to have someone at the top that they like; it just makes all the difference. And Hugh thinks it so hopeful that they turned you out of St. Gregory's; he doesn't entirely approve of St. Gregory's, as you know. Now will you?"

Eddy, after due consideration, said he would do the best he could.

"I shall be very inept, you know. Will it matter much? I suppose the men down there—Pollard and the rest—will see me through. And you'll be coming down sometimes, perhaps."

She said "I may," then looked at him for a moment speculatively, and added, "But I may not. I might be away, with Hugh."

"Oh," said Eddy.

"If no one else satisfactory can go with him," she said. "He must have the right person. Someone who, besides looking after him, will make him like living and travelling and seeing things. That's very important, the doctor says. He is such a terribly depressed person, poor Hugh. I can brighten him up. So I rather expect I will go, and walk about Greece with him. We would both like it, of course."

"Of course," said Eddy, his chin on his hand, looking out of the window at the orange trees that grew in tubs by the door.

"And, lest we should have people shocked," added Eileen, "Bridget's coming too. Not that we mind people with that sort of horrible mind being shocked—but it wouldn't do to spoil Hugh's work by it, and it might. Hugh, of course, doesn't want things said about me, either. People are so stupid. I wonder will the time ever come when two friends can go about together the way no harm will be said. Bridget thinks never. But after all, if no one's prepared to set an example of common-sense, how are we to move on ever out of all this horrid, improper tangle and muddle? Jane, of course, says, what does it matter, no one who counts would mind; but then for Jane so few people count. Jane would do it herself to-morrow, and never even suspect that anyone was shocked. But one can't have people saying things about Hugh, and he running clubs and settlements and things; it would destroy him and them; he's one of the people who've got to be careful; which is a bore, but can't be helped."

"No, it can't be helped," Eddy agreed. "One doesn't want people to be hurt or shocked, even apart from clubs and things; and so many even of the nicest people would be."

There she differed from him. "Not the nicest. The less nice. The foolish, the coarse-minded, the shut-in, the—the tiresome."

Eddy smiled disagreement, and she remembered that they would be shocked at the Deanery, doubtless.

"Ah well," she said, "have it your own way. The nicest, then, as well as the least nice, because none of them know any better, poor dears. For that matter, Bridget said she'd be shocked herself if we went alone. Bridget has moods, you know, when she prides herself on being proper—the British female guarding the conventions. She's in one of them now.... Well, go and see Hugh to-morrow, will you, and talk about the Settlement. He'll have a lot to say, but don't have him excited. It's wonderful what a trust he has in you, Eddy, since you left St. Gregory's."

"An inadequate reason," said Eddy, "but leading to a very proper conclusion. Yes, I'll go and see him, then."

He did so, next day. He found Datcherd at the writing-table in his library. It was a large and beautiful library in a large and beautiful house. The Datcherds were rich (or would have been had not Datcherd spent much too much money on building houses for the poor, and Lady Dorothy Datcherd rather too much on cards and clothes and other luxuries), and there was about their belongings that air of caste, of inherited culture, of transmitted intelligence and recognition of social and political responsibilities, that is perhaps only to be found in families with a political tradition of several generations. Datcherd wasn't a clever literary free-lance; he was a hereditary Whig; that was why he couldn't be detached, why, about his breaking with custom and convention, there would always be a wrench and strain, a bitterness of hostility, instead of the light ease of Eileen Le Moine's set, that could gently mock at the heavy-handed world because it had never been under its dominance, never conceived anything but freedom. That, and because of their finer sense of responsibility, is why it is aristocrats who will always make the best social revolutionaries. They know that life is real, life is earnest; they are bound up with the established status by innumerable ties, which either to keep or to break means purpose. They are, in fact, heavily involved, all round; they cannot escape their liabilities; they are the grown-up people in a light-hearted world of children. Surely, then, they should have more of the reins in their hands, less jerking of them from below.... Such, at least, were Eddy's reflections in Datcherd's library, while he waited for Datcherd to finish a letter and thought how ill he looked.

Their ensuing conversation need not be detailed. Datcherd told Eddy about arranging lectures at the Club House whenever he could, about the reading-room, the gymnasium, the billiard-room, the woodwork, and the other diversions and educational enterprises which flourish in such institutions. Eddy was familiar with them already, having sometimes been down to the Club House. It was in its main purpose educational. To it came youths between the ages of fifteen and five and twenty, and gave their evenings to acquiring instruction in political economy, sociology, history, art, physical exercises, science, and other branches of learning. They had regular instructors; and besides these, irregular lecturers came down once or twice a week, friends of Datcherd's, politicians, social workers, writers, anyone who would come and was considered by Datcherd suitable. The Fabian Society, it seemed, throve still among the Club members, and was given occasional indulgences such as Mr. Shaw or Mr. Sidney Webb, and lesser treats frequently. They had debates, and other habits such as will be readily imagined. Having indicated these, Datcherd proceeded to tell Eddy something about his assistant workers, in what ways each needed firm or tender handling.

While they were talking, Billy Raymond came in, to tell Datcherd about a new poet he had found, who wrote verse that seemed suitable for *Further*. Billy Raymond, a generous and appreciative person, was given to finding new poets, usually in cellars, attics, or workmen's flats. It was commonly said that he less found them than made them, by some transmuting magic of his own touch. Anyhow they quite often produced poetry, for longer or shorter periods. This latest one was a Socialist in conviction and expression; hence his suitability for *Further*. Eddy wasn't sure that they ought to talk of *Further*; it obviously had Hugh excited.

He and Billy Raymond came away together, which rather pleased Eddy, as he liked Billy better than most people of his acquaintance, which was saying much. There was a breadth about Billy, a large and gentle tolerance, a courtesy towards all sorts and conditions of men and views, that made him restful, as compared, for instance, with the intolerant Arnold Denison. Perhaps the difference was partly that Billy was a poet, with the artist's vision, which takes in, and Arnold only a critic, whose function it is to select and exclude. Billy, in short, was a producer, and Arnold a publisher; and publishers have to be for ever saying that things won't do, aren't good enough. If they can't say that, they are poor publishers indeed. Billy, in Eddy's view, approached more nearly than most people to that synthesis which, Eddy believed, unites all factions and all sections of truth.

Billy said, "Poor dear Hugh. I am extraordinarily sorry for him. I am glad you are going to help in the Settlement. He hates leaving it so much. I'm sure I couldn't worry about my work or anything else if I was going to walk about Greece for a month; but he's so—so ascetic. I think I respect Datcherd more than almost anyone; he's so absolutely single-minded. He won't enjoy Greece a bit, I believe, because of all the people in slums who can't be there, and wouldn't if they could. It will seem to him wicked waste of money. Waste, you know! My word!"

"Perhaps," said Eddy, "he'll learn how to enjoy life more now his wife has left him. She must have been a weight on his mind."

"Oh, well," said Billy, "I don't know. Perhaps so.... One never really felt that she quite existed, and I daresay he didn't either, so I don't suppose her being gone will make so very much difference. She was a sort of unreal thing—a shadow. I always got on with her pretty well; in fact, I rather liked her in a way; but I never felt she was actually there."

"She'd be there to Datcherd, though," Eddy said, feeling that Billy's wisdom hardly embraced the peculiar circumstances of married life, and Billy, never much interested in personal relations, said, "Perhaps."

They were in Kensington, and Billy went to call on his grandmother, who lived in Gordon Place, and to whom he went frequently to play backgammon and relate the news. Billy was a very affectionate and dutiful young man, and also nearly as fond of backgammon as his grandmother was. With his grandmother lived an aunt, who didn't care for his poetry much, and Billy was very fond of her too. He sometimes went with his grandmother to St. Mary Abbot's Church, to help her to see weddings (which she preferred even to backgammon), or attend services. She was proud of Billy, but, for poets to read, preferred Scott, Keble, or Doctor Watts. She admitted herself behind modern times, but loved to see and hear what young people were doing, though it usually seemed rather silly. To her Billy went this afternoon, and Eddy meanwhile called on Mrs. Le Moine and Miss Hogan in Campden Hill Road. He found Miss Hogan in, just returned from a picture-show, and she gave him tea and conversation.

"Of course you've heard all about our intentions. Actually we're off on Thursday.... Last time Eileen went abroad, the people she was with took a maniac by mistake; so very uncomfortable. I quite thought after that she had decided that travel was not for her. However, it seems not. You know—I'm sure she told you—she was for going just he and she, *tout simple*. Most improper, of course, not to say unwholesome. They meant no harm, dear children, but who would believe that, and even so, what are the *convenances* for but to be observed? I put it before Eileen in my most banal and *borné* manner, but, needless to say, how fruitless! So at last I had to offer to go too. Of course from kindness she had to accept that, though it won't be at all the same, particularly not to Hugh. Anyhow there we are, and we're off on Thursday. Hugh will be very much upset by the Channel; I believe he always is; no constitution whatever, poor creature. Also I believe he is of those with whom it lasts on between Calais and Paris—a most unhappy class, but to be avoided as travelling companions. I know too well, because of an aunt of mine.... Well, anyhow we're going to take the train to Trieste, and then a ship to Kalamata, and then take to our feet and walk across Greece. Hitherto I have only done Greece on the Dunnottar Castle, in the care of Sir Henry Lunn, which, if less thrilling, is safer, owing to the wild dogs that tear the pedestrian on the Greek hills, one is given to understand. I only hope we may be preserved.... And meanwhile you're going to run those wonderful clubs of Hugh's. I wonder if you'll do it at all as he would wish! It is beautiful to see how he trusts you—why, I can't imagine. In his place I wouldn't; I would rather hand over my clubs to some unlettered subordinate after my own heart and bred in my own faith. As for you, you have so many faiths that Hugh's will be swamped in the crowd. But you feel confident that you will do it well? That is good, and the main qualification for success."

Thus Miss Hogan babbled on, partly because she always did, partly because the young man looked rather strained, and she was afraid if she paused that he might say how sad he was at Eileen's going, and she believed these things better unexpressed. He wasn't the only young man who was fond of Eileen, and Miss Hogan had her own ideas as to how to deal with such emotions. She didn't believe it went deep with Eddy, or that he would admit to himself any emotion at all beyond friendship, owing to his own views as to what was right, not to speak of what was sensible; and no doubt if left to himself for a month or so, he would manage to recover entirely. It would be so obviously silly, as well as wrong, to fall in love with Eileen Le Moine, and Bridget did not believe Eddy, in spite of some confusion in his mental outlook, to be really silly.

She directed the conversation on to the picture-show she had just been to, and that reminded her of Sally Peters.

"Did you hear what the stupid child's done? Joined the Wild Women, and jabbed her umbrella into a lot of Post Impressionists in the Grafton Galleries. Of course they caught her at it—the clumsiest child!—and took her up on the spot, and she's coming up for trial to-morrow with three other lunatics, old enough to know better than to lead an ignorant baby like that into mischief. I expect she'll get a month, and serve her right. I suppose she'll go on hunger-strike; but she's so plump that it will probably affect her health not unfavourably. I don't know who got hold of her; doubtless some mad and bad creatures who saw she had no more sense than a little owl, and set her blundering into shop-windows and picture-glasses like a young blue-bottle.... By the way, though you are, I know, so many things, I feel sure you draw the line at the militants."

Eddy said he thought he saw their point of view.

"Point of view! They've not one," Miss Hogan cried. "I suppose, like other decent people, you want women to have votes! Well, you must grant they've spoilt any chance of *that*, anyhow—smashed up the whole suffrage campaign with their horrible jabbing umbrellas and absurd little bombs."

Eddy granted that. "They've smashed the suffrage, for the present, yes. Poor things." He reflected for a moment on these unfortunate persons, and added, "But I do see what they mean, all the same. They smash and spoil and hurt things and people and causes, because they are stupid with anger; but they've got things to be angry about, after all. Oh, I admit they're very, very stupid and inartistic, and hopelessly unaesthetic and British and unimaginative and cruel and without any humour at all—but I do see what they mean, in a way."

"Well, don't explain it to me, then, because I've heard it at first-hand far too often lately."

Eddy went round to the rooms in Old Compton Street which he shared with Arnold Denison. Arnold had chosen Soho for residence partly because he liked it, partly to improve his knowledge of languages, and partly to study the taste of the neighbourhood in literature, as it was there that he intended, when he had more leisure, to start a bookshop. Eddy, too, liked it. (This is a superfluous observation, because anybody would.) In fact, he liked his life in general just now. He liked reviewing for the *Daily Post* and writing for himself (himself *via* the editors of various magazines who met with his productions on their circular route and pushed them on again). He liked getting review copies of books to keep; his taste was catholic and omnivorous, and boggled at nothing. With joy he perused everything, even novels which had won prizes in novel competitions, popular discursive works called "About the Place," and books of verse (to do them justice, not even popular) called "Pipings," and such. He wrote appreciative reviews of all of them, because he appreciated them all. It may fairly be said that he saw each as its producer saw it, which may or may not be what a reviewer should try to do, but is anyhow grateful and comforting to the reviewed. Arnold, who did not do this, in vain protested that he would lose his job soon. "No literary editor will stand such indiscriminate fulsomeness for long.... It's a dispensation of providence that you didn't come and read for us, as I once mistakenly wished. You would, so far as your advice carried any weight, have dragged us down into the gutter. Have you no sense of values or of decency? Can you really like these florid effusions of base minds?" He was reading through Eddy's last review, which was of a book of verse by a lady gifted with emotional tendencies and an admiration for landscape. Arnold shook his head and laughed as he put the review down.

"The queer thing about it is that it's not a bad review, in spite of everything you say in appreciation of the lunatic who wrote the book. That's what I can't understand; how you can be so intelligent and yet so idiotic. You've given the book exactly, in a few phrases—no one could possibly mistake its nature—and then you make several quite true, not to say brilliant remarks about it—and then you go on and say how good it is.... Well, I shall be interested to see how long they keep you on."

"They like me," Eddy assured him, complacently. "They think I write well. The authors like me, too. Many a heartfelt letter of thanks do I get from those whom there are few to praise and fewer still to love. As you may have noticed, they strew the breakfast table. Is it *comme il faut* for me to answer? I do—I mean, I did, both times—because it seemed politer, but it was perhaps a mistake, because the correspondence between me and one of them has not ceased yet, and possibly never will, since neither of us likes to end it. How involving life is!"

Meanwhile he went to the Club House by the Lea most evenings. That, too, he liked. He had a gift which Datcherd had detected in him, the gift of getting on well with all sorts of people, irrespective of their incomes, breeding, social status, intelligence, or respectability. He did not, like Arnold, rule out the unintelligent, the respectable, the commonplace; nor, like Datcherd, the orthodoxly religious; nor, as Jane did, without knowing it, the vulgar; nor, like many delightful and companionable and well-bred people, the uneducated, those whom we, comprehensively and rightly, call the poor—rightly, because, though poverty may seem the merest superficial and insignificant attribute of the completed product, it is also the original, fundamental cause of all the severing differences. Molly Bellairs thought Eddy would have made a splendid clergyman, a better one than his father, who was unlimitedly kind, but ill at ease, and talked above poor people's heads. Eddy, with less grip of theological problems, had a surer hold of points of view, and apprehended the least witty of jokes, the least pathetic of quarrels, the least picturesque of emotions. Hence he was popular.

He found that the sort of lectures Datcherd's clubs were used to expect were largely on subjects like the Minimum Wage, Capitalism versus Industrialism, Organised Labour, the Eight Hours Day, Poor Law Reform, the Endowment of Mothers, Co-partnership, and such; all very interesting and profitable if well treated. So Eddy wrote to Bob Traherne, the second curate at St. Gregory's, to ask him to give one. Traherne replied that he would, if Eddy liked, give a course of six. He proceeded to do so, and as he was a good, concise, and pungent speaker, drew large audiences and was immensely popular. At the end of his lecture he sold penny tracts by Church Socialists; really sold them, in large numbers. After his third lecture, which was on the Minimum Wage, he said he would be glad to receive the names of any persons who would like to join the Church Socialist League, the most effective society he knew of for furthering these objects. He received seven forthwith, and six more after the next.

Protests reached Eddy from a disturbed secretary, a pale, red-haired young man, loyal to Datcherd's spirit.

"It's not what Mr. Datcherd would like, Mr. Oliver."

Eddy said, "Why on earth shouldn't he? He likes the men to be Socialists, doesn't he?"

"Not that sort, he doesn't. At least, he wouldn't. He likes them to think for themselves, not to be tied up with the Church."

"Well, they are thinking for themselves. He wouldn't like them to be tied up to his beliefs either, surely. I feel sure it's all right, Pollard. Anyhow, I can't stop them joining the League if they want to, can I?"

"We ought to stop the Reverend Traherne that's where it is. He'd talk the head off an elephant. He gets a hold of them, and abuses it. It isn't right, and it isn't fair, nor what Mr. Datcherd would like in the Club."

"Nonsense," said Eddy. "Mr. Datcherd would be delighted. Mr. Traherne's a first-rate lecturer, you know; they learn more from him than they do from all the Socialist literature they get out of the library."

Worse than this, several young men who despised church-going, quite suddenly took to it, bicycling over to the Borough to hear the Reverend Traherne preach. Datcherd had no objection to anyone going to church if from conviction, but this sort of unbalanced, unreasoning yielding to a personal influence he would certainly consider degrading and unworthy of a thinking citizen. Be a man's convictions what they might, Datcherd held, let them *be* convictions, based on reason and principle, not incoherent impulses and chance emotions. It was almost certain that he would not have approved of Traherne's influence over his clubs.

Still less, Pollard thought, would he have approved of Captain Greville's. Captain Greville was a retired captain, who needs no description here. His mission in life was to talk about the National Service League. Eddy, who, it may be remembered, belonged among other leagues to this, met him somewhere, and requested him to come and address the club on the subject one evening. He did so. He made a very good speech, for thirty-five minutes, which is exactly the right length for this topic. (Some people err, and speak too long, on this as on many other subjects, and miss their goal in consequence.) Captain Greville said, How delightful to strengthen the national fibre and the sense of civic duty by bringing all men into relation with national ideas through personal training during youth; to strengthen the national health by sound physical development and discipline, etcetera; to bring to bear upon the most important business with which a nation can have to deal, namely, National Defence, the knowledge, the interest, and the criticism of the national mind; to safeguard the nation against war by showing that we are prepared for it, and ensure that, should war break out, peace may be speedily re-established; in short, to Organize our Man Power; further, not to be shot in time of invasion for carrying a gun unlawfully, which is a frequent incident (sensation). He said a good deal more, which need not be specified, as it is doubtless familiar to many, and would be unwelcome to others. At the end he said, "Are you Democrats? Then join the League, which advocates the only democratic system of defence. Are you Socialists?" (this was generous, because he disliked Socialists very much) "Then join the League, which aims at a reform strictly in accordance with the principles of co-operative socialism; in fact, many people base their opposition to it on the grounds that it is too socialistic. Finally (he observed), what we want is not a standing army, and not a war—God forbid—but men capable of fighting *like* men in defence of their wives, their children, and their homes."

The Club apparently realised suddenly that this was what they did want, and crowded up to sign cards and receive buttons inscribed with the inspiring motto: "The Path of Duty is the Path of Safety." In short, quite a third of the young men became adherents of the League, encouraged thereto by Eddy, and congratulated by the enthusiastic captain. They were invited to ask questions, so they did. They asked, What about employers chucking a man for good because he had to be away for his four months camp? Answer: This would not happen; force would be exerted over the employer. (Some scepticism, but a general sentiment of approval for this, as for something which would indeed be grand if it could be worked, and which might in itself be worth joining the League for, merely to score off the employer.) Further answer: The late Sir Joseph Whitworth said, "The labour of a man who has gone through a course of military drill is worth eighteen-pence a week more than that of one untrained, as through the training received in military drill men learn ready obedience, attention, and combination, all of which are so necessary in work." Question: Would they get it? Answer: Get what? Question: The eighteen-pence. Answer: In justice they certainly should. Question: Would employers be forced to give it them? Answer: All these details are left to be worked out later in the Bill. Conclusion: The Bill would not be popular among employers. Further conclusion: Let us join it. Which they did.

Before he departed, Captain Greville said that he was very pleased with the encouraging results of the evening, and he hoped that as many as would be interested would come and see a cinematograph display he was giving in Hackney next week, called "In Time of Invasion." From that he would venture to say they would learn something of the horrors of unprepared attack. The Club went to that. It was a splendid show, well worth threepence. It abounded in men being found unlawfully with guns and being shot like rabbits; in untrained and incompetent soldiers fleeing from the foe; abandoned mothers defending their cottage homes to the last against a brutal soldiery; corpses of children tossed on pikes to make a Prussian holiday; Boy Scouts and Girl Guides, the one saving element in the terrible display of national incompetence, performing marvellous feats of skill and heroism, and dying like flies in discharge of their duties. Afterwards there was a very different series to illustrate the

Invasion as it would be had the National Service Act been passed. "The Invaders realise their Mistake," was inscribed on the preliminary curtain. Well-trained, efficient, and courageous young men then sallied into the field, proud in the possession of fire-arms they had a right to, calm in their perfect training, temerity, and discipline, presenting an unflinching and impregnable front to the cowering foe, who retreated in broken disorder, realising their mistake (cheers). Then on the Finis curtain blazed out the grand moral of it all: "The Path of Duty is the Path of Safety. Keep your homes inviolate by learning to Defend them." (Renewed cheers, and "God Save the King").

A very fine show, to which, it may be added, Mr. Sidney Pollard, the Club Secretary, did not go.

It was soon after this that Captain Greville, having been much pleased—very pleased, as he said—by the Lea-side Club, presented its library with a complete set of Kipling. Kipling, since the Kipling period was some years past, was not well known by the Club; appearing among them suddenly, on the top of the Cinema, he made something of a furore. If Mr. Datcherd would get *him* to write poetry for *Further*, now, instead of Mr. Henderson and Mr. Raymond, and all the people he did get, that would be something like. Finding Kipling so popular, and yielding to a request, Eddy, who read rather well, gave some Kipling readings, which were much enjoyed by a crowded audience.

"Might as well take them to a music hall at once," complained Mr. Pollard.

"Would they like it? I will," returned Eddy, and did so, paying for a dozen boys at the Empire.

It must not be supposed that Eddy neglected, in the cult of a manly patriotism, the other aspects of life. On the contrary, he induced Billy Raymond, a good-natured person, to give a lecture on the Drama, and after it, took a party to the Savoy Theatre, to see Granville Barker's Shakespeare, which bored them a good deal. Then he got Jane to give an address on drawings, and, to illustrate it, took some rather apathetic youths to see Jane's own exhibition. Also he conducted a party to where Mr. Roger Fry was speaking on Post-Impressionism, and then, when they had thoroughly grasped it, to the gallery where it was just then being exemplified. First he told them that they could laugh at the pictures if they choose, of course, but that was an exceedingly stupid way of looking at them; so they actually did not, such was his influence over them at this time. Instead, when he pointed out to them the beauties of Matisse, they pretended to agree with him, and listened tolerant, if bored, while he had an intelligent discussion with an artist friend whom he met.

All this is to say that Eddy had his young men well in hand—better in hand than Datcherd, who was less cordial and hail-fellow-well-met with them, had ever had them. It was great fun. Influencing people in a mass always is; it feels rather like driving a large and powerful car, which is sent swerving to right or left by a small turn of the wrist. Probably actors feel like this when acting, only more so; perhaps speakers feel like this when speaking. Doing what you like with people, the most interesting and absorbing of the plastic materials ready to the hand—that is better than working with clay, paints, or words. Not that Eddy was consciously aware of what he was doing in that way; only about each fresh thing as it turned up he was desirous to make these lads that he liked feel keen and appreciative, as he felt himself; and he was delighted that they did so, showing themselves thereby so sane, sensible, and intelligent. He had found them keen enough on some important things—industrial questions, certain aspects of Socialism, the Radical Party in politics; it was for him to make them equally keen on other things, hitherto apparently rather overlooked by them. One of these things was the Church; here his success was only partial, but distinctly encouraging. Another was the good in Toryism, which they were a little blind to. To open their eyes, he had a really intelligent Conservative friend of his to address them on four successive Tuesdays on politics. He did not want in the least to change their politics—what can be better than to be a Radical?—(this was as well, because it would have been a task outside even his sphere of influence)—but certainly they should see both sides. So both sides were set before them; and the result was certainly that they looked much less intolerantly than before upon the wrong side, because Mr. Oliver, who was a first-rater, gave it his countenance, as he had to Matisse and that tedious thing at the Savoy. Matisse, Shakespeare, Tariff Reform, they all seemed silly, but there, they pleased a good chap and a pleasant friend, who could also appreciate Harry Lauder, old Victor Grayson, Kipling, and the Minimum Wage.

Such were the interests of a varied and crowded life on club nights by the Lea. Distraught by them, Mr. Sidney Pollard wrote to his master in Greece—(address, Poste-Restante, Athens, where eventually his wanderings would lead him and he would call for letters)—to say that all was going to sixes and sevens, and here was a Tariff Reformer let loose on the Club on Tuesday evenings, and a parson to rot about his fancy Socialism on Wednesdays, and another parson holding a mission service in the street last Sunday afternoon, not even about Socialism—(this was Father Dempsey)—and half the club hanging about him and asking him posers, which is always the beginning of the end, because any parson, having been bred to it, can answer posers so much more posingly than anyone can ask them; and some captain or other talking that blanked nonsense about National Service, and giving round his silly buttons as if they were chocolate drops at a school-feast, and leading them on to go to an idiot Moving Picture Show, calculated to turn them all into Jingoes of the deepest dye; and some Blue Water maniac gassing about Dreadnoughts, so that "We want eight and we won't wait" was sung by the school-children in the streets instead of "Every nice girl loves a sailor," which may mean, emotionally, much the same, but is politically offensive. Further, Mr. Oliver had been giving Kipling readings, and half the lads were Kipling-mad, and fought to get Barrack-room Ballads out of the library. Finally, "Mr. Oliver may mean no harm, but he is doing a lot," said Mr. Pollard. "If he goes on here, the tone of the Club will be spoilt, he is personally popular, owing to being a friend to all in his manner and having pleasant ways, and that is the worst sort. If you are not coming home yourself soon, perhaps you will make some change by writing, and tell Mr. Oliver if you approve of above things or not. I have thought it right to let you know all, and you will act according as you think. I very much trust your health is on the mend, you are badly missed here."

Datcherd got that letter at last, but not just yet, for he was then walking inland across the Plain of Thessaly between Volo and Tempe.

CHAPTER X.

DATCHERD'S RETURN.

ON the last day of April, Eddy procured an Irish Nationalist to address the Club on Home Rule. He was a hot-tempered person, and despised English people and said so; which was foolish in a speaker, and rather discounted his other remarks, because the Club young men preferred to be liked, even by those who made speeches to them. His cause, put no doubt over-vehemently, was on the whole approved of by the Club, Radically inclined as it in the main was; but it is a noticeable fact that this particular subject is apt to fall dead on English working-class audiences, who have, presumably, a deeply-rooted feeling that it does not seriously affect them either way. Anyhow, this Nationalist hardly evoked the sympathy he deserved in the Club. Also they were inclined to be amused at his accent, which was unmodified Wexford. Probably Eddy appreciated him and his arguments more than anyone else did.

So, when on the second day of May Eddy introduced an Orangeman to speak on the same subject from another point of view, the audience was inclined to receive him favourably. The Orangeman was young, much younger than the Nationalist, and equally Irish, though from another region, both geographically and socially. His accent, what he had of it, is best described as polite North of Ireland, and he had been at Cambridge with Eddy. Though capable of fierceness, and with an Ulster-will-fight look in the eye, the fierceness was directed rather against his disloyal compatriots than against his audience, which was more satisfactory to the audience. And whenever he liked he could make them laugh, which was more satisfactory still. From his face you might, before he spoke, guess him to be a Nationalist, so essentially and indubitably south-west Irish was the look of it. To avert so distressing an error he did speak, as a rule, quite a lot.

He spoke this evening with energy, lucidity, humour, and vehemence, and the Club listened appreciatively. Gradually he worked them up from personal approval of himself to partial approval of, or at least sympathy with, his cause. He went into the financial question with an imposing production of figures. He began several times, "The Nationalists will tell ycu," and then proceeded to repeat precisely what the Nationalist the other night *had* told them, only to knock it down with an argument that was sometimes conclusive, often would just do, and occasionally just wouldn't; and the Club cheered the first sort, accepted the second as ingenious, and said "Oh," good-humouredly, to the third. Altogether it was an excellent speech, full of profound conviction, with some incontrovertible sense, and a smattering of intelligent nonsense. Not a word was dull, and not a word was unkind to the Pope of Rome or his adherents, as is usual, and perhaps essential, in such speeches when produced in Ireland, and necessitates their careful expurgating before they are delivered to English audiences, who have a tolerant, if supercilious, feeling towards that misguided Church. The young man spoke for half an hour, and held his audience. He held them even when he said, drawing to the end, "I wonder do any of you here know anything at all about Ireland and Irish politics, or do you get it all second-hand from the English Radical papers? Do you know at all what you're talking about? Bad government, incompetent economy, partiality, prejudice, injustice, tyranny—that's what the English Radicals want to hand us over to. And that is what they will not hand us over to, because we in Ulster, the most truly and nationally Irish part of Ireland, have signed this." He produced from his breast-pocket the Covenant, and held it up before them, so that they all saw the Red Hand that blazed out on it. He read it through to them, and sat down. Cheers broke out, stamping of feet, clapping of hands; it was the most enthusiastic reception a speaker had ever had at the Club.

Someone began singing "Rule Britannia," as the nearest expression that occurred to him of the patriotic and anti-disruptive sentiments that filled him, and it was taken up and shouted all over the room. It was as if the insidious influence of Kipling, the National Service League, the Invasion Pictures, the Primrose League, and the Blue Water School, which had been eating with gradual corruption into the sound heart of the Club, was breaking out at last, under the finishing poison of Orangeism, into an eruption which could only be eased by song and shout. So they sang and shouted, some from enthusiasm, some for fun, and Eddy said to his friend the speaker, "You've fairly fetched them this time," and looked smiling over the jubilant crowd, from the front chairs to the back, and, at the back of all, met the eyes of Datcherd. He stood leaning against the door, unjubilant, songless, morose, his hands in his pockets, a cynical smile faintly touching his lips. At his side was Sidney Pollard, with very bright eyes in a white face, and a "There, you see for yourself" air about him.

Eddy hadn't known Datcherd was coming down to the Club to-night, though he knew he had arrived in England, three weeks before he had planned. Seeing him, he rose to his feet and smiled, and the audience, following his eyes, turned round and saw their returned president and master. Upon that they cheered again, louder if possible than before. Datcherd's acknowledgment was of the faintest. He stood there for a moment longer, then turned and left the room.

The meeting ended, after the usual courtesies and votes of thanks, and Eddy took his friend away.

"You must come and be introduced to Datcherd," he said. "I wonder where he's got to."

His friend looked doubtful. "He could have come and spoken to me in the room if he'd wanted. Perhaps he didn't. Perhaps he'd be tired after his journey. He didn't look extraordinarily cheery, somehow. I think I'll not bother him."

"Oh, he's all right. He only looked like a Home Ruler listening to Orange cheering. I expect they don't, as a rule, look very radiant, do they?"

"They do not. But you don't mean he'd mind my coming to speak, surely? Because, if he does, I ought never to have come. You told me they had lectures from all sorts of people on all sorts of things."

"So they do. No, of course he wouldn't mind. But that's the way he's bound to look in public, as a manifesto, don't you see. Like a clergyman listening to a Nonconformist preacher. He has to assert his principles."

"But a Church clergyman probably wouldn't get a Nonconformist to preach in his church. They don't, I believe, as a rule."

Eddy was forced to admit that, unfortunately, they didn't.

His friend, a person of good manners, was a little cross. "We've had him offended now, and I don't blame him. You should have told me. I should never have come. It's such rustic manners, to break into a person's Club and preach things he hates. I could tell he hated it, by the look in his eye. He kept the other end of the room, the way he wouldn't break out at me and say anything ferocious. No, I'm not coming to look for him; I wouldn't dare look him in the face; you can go by yourself. You've fairly let me in, Oliver. I hate being rude to the wrong side, it gives them such an advantage. They're rude enough to us, as a rule, to do for the two. *I* don't want to have anything to do with his little Radical Club; if he wants to keep it to himself and his Radical friends, he's welcome."

"You're talking nonsense," Eddy said. "Did it behave like a Radical club to-night?"

"It did not. Which is exactly why Datcherd has every reason to be annoyed. Well, you can tell him from me that it was no one's fault but your own. Good-night."

He departed, more in anger than in sorrow—(it had really been rather fun to-night, though rude)—and Eddy went to find Datcherd.

But he didn't find Datcherd. He was told that Datcherd had left the Club and gone home. His friend's remark came back to him. "He kept the other end of the room, the way he wouldn't break out at me and say anything ferocious." Was that what Datcherd was doing to him, or was he tired after his journey? Eddy hoped for the best, but felt forebodings. Datcherd certainly had not looked cordial or cheerful. The way he had looked had disappointed and rather hurt the Club. They felt that another expression, after three months absence, would have been more suitable. After all, for pleasantness of demeanour, Mr. Datcherd, even at the best of times (which this, it seemed, hardly was) wasn't a patch on Mr. Oliver.

These events occurred on a Friday evening. It so happened that Eddy was going out of town next morning for a Cambridge week-end, so he would not see Datcherd till Monday evening. He and Arnold spent the week-end at Arnold's home. Whenever Eddy visited the Denisons he was struck afresh by the extreme and rarefied refinement of their atmosphere; they (except Arnold, who had been coarsened, like himself, by contact with the world) were academic in the best sense; theoretical, philosophical, idealistic, serenely sure of truth, making up in breeding what, possibly, they a little lacked (at least Mrs. Denison and her daughter lacked) in humour; never swerving from the political, religious, and economic position they had taken up once and for all. A trifle impenetrable and closed to new issues, they were; the sort of Liberal one felt would never, however changed the circumstances, become Conservative. A valuable type, representing breeding and conscience in a rough-and-tumble world; if Christian and Anglican, it often belongs to the Christian Social Union; if not, like the Denisons, it will surely belong to some other well-intentioned and high-principled society for bettering the poor. They are, in brief, gentlemen and ladies. Life in the country is too sleepy for them and their progressive ideas; London is quite too wide awake; so they flourish like exquisite flowers in our older Universities and in Manchester, and visit Greece and Italy in the vacations.

Eddy found it peaceful to be with the Denisons. To come back to London on Monday morning was a little disturbing. He could not help a slight feeling of anxiety about his meeting with Datcherd. Perhaps it was just as well, he thought, to have given Datcherd two days to recover from the shock of the Unionist meeting. He hoped that Datcherd, when he met him, would look less like a Home Ruler listening to Orange cheering (a very unpleasant expression of countenance) than he had on Friday evening. Thinking that he might as well find out about this as soon as possible, he called at Datcherd's house that afternoon.

Datcherd was in his library, as usual, writing. He got up and shook hands with Eddy, and said, "I was coming round to see you," which relieved Eddy. But he spoke rather gravely, and added, "There are some things I want to talk to you about," and sat down and nursed his gaunt knee in his thin hands and gnawed his lips.

Eddy asked him if he was much better, thinking he didn't look it, and if he had had a good time. Datcherd scarcely answered; he was one of those people who only think of one thing at once, and he was thinking just now of something other than his health or his good time.

He said, after a moment's silence, "It's been extremely kind of you to manage the Club all this time."

Eddy, with a wan smile, said apologetically, "You know, we really did have a Home Ruler to speak on Wednesday."

Datcherd relaxed a little, and smiled in his turn.

"I know. In fact, I gather that there are very few representatives of any causes whatever whom you have *not* had to speak."

"I see," said Eddy, "that Pollard has told you all."

"Pollard has told me some things. And you must remember that I spent both Saturday and Sunday evenings at the Club."

"What," inquired Eddy hopefully, "did you think of it?"

Datcherd was silent for a moment. Perhaps he was remembering again how kind it had been of Eddy to manage the Club all this time. When he spoke, it was with admirable moderation.

"It hardly," he said, "seems quite on the lines I left it on. I was a little surprised, I must own. We had a very small Club on Sunday night, because a lot of them had gone off to some service in church. That surprised me rather. They never used to do that. Of course I don't mind, but——"

"That's Traherne," said Eddy. "He got a tremendous hold on some of them when he came down to speak. He's always popular, you know, with men and lads."

"I daresay. What made you get him?"

"Oh, to speak about rents and wages and things. He's very good. They liked him."

"That is apparent. He's dragged some of them into the Church Socialist League, and more to church after him. Well, it's their own business, of course; if they like the sort of thing, I've no objection. They'll get tired of it soon, I expect.... But, if you'll excuse my asking, why on earth have you been corrupting their minds with lectures on Tariff Reform, National Service, Ulsterism and Dreadnoughts? Didn't you realise that one can't let in that sort of influence without endangering the sanity of a set of half-educated lads? I left them reading Mill; I find them reading Kipling. Upon my word, anyone would think you belonged to the Primrose League, from the way you've been going on."

"I do," said Eddy simply.

Datcherd stared at him, utterly taken aback.

"You *what*?"

"I belong to the Primrose League," Eddy repeated. "Why shouldn't I?"

Datcherd pulled his startled wits together, and laughed shortly.

"I beg your pardon. The mistake, I suppose, was mine. I had somehow got it into my head that you were a Fabian."

"So I am," said Eddy, patiently explaining. "All those old things, you know. And most of the new ones as well. I'm sorry if you didn't know; I suppose I ought to have mentioned it, but I never thought about it. Does it matter?"

Datcherd was gazing at him with grave, startled eyes, as at a maniac.

"Matter? Well, I don't know. Yes, I suppose it would have mattered, from my point of view, if I'd known. Because it just means that you've been playing when I thought you were in earnest; that, whereas I supposed you took your convictions and mine seriously and meant to act on them, really they're just a game to you. You take no cause seriously, I suppose."

"I take all causes seriously," Eddy corrected him quickly. He got up, and walked about the room, his hands deep in his pockets, frowning a little because life was so serious.

"You see," he explained, stopping in front of Datcherd and frowning down on him, "truth is so pervasive; it gets everywhere; leaks into everything. Like cod-liver oil spilt in a trunk of clothes; everything's saturated with it. (Is that a nasty comparison? I thought of it because it happened to me the other day.) The clothes are all different from each other, but the cod-liver oil is in all of them for ever and ever. Truth is like that—pervasive. Isn't it?"

"No," said Datcherd, with vehemence. "No. Truth is *not* like that. If it were, it would mean that one thing was no better and no worse than another; that all progress, moral and otherwise, was illusive. We should all become fatalists, torpid, uncaring, dead, sitting with our hands before us and drifting with the tide. There'd be an end of all fight, all improvement, all life. But truth is *not* like that. One thing *is* better than another, and always will be. Democracy *is* a better aim than oligarchy; freedom *is* better than tyranny; work *is* better than idleness. And, because it fights, however slowly and hesitatingly, on the side of those better things, Liberalism is better than Toryism, the League of Young Liberals a better thing to encourage among the young men of the country than the Primrose League. You say truth is everywhere. Frankly, I look at the Primrose League, and all your Tory Associations, and I can't find it. I see only a monumental tissue of lies. Lying to the people for their good—that's what all honest Tories would admit they do. Lying to them for their harm—that's what we say they do. Truth! It isn't named among them. They've not got minds that can know truth when they see it. It's not their fault. They're mostly good men warped by a bad creed. And you say one creed is as good as another."

"I say there's truth in all of them," said Eddy. "Can't you see the truth in Toryism? I can, so clearly. It's all so hackneyed, so often repeated, but it's true in spite of that. Isn't there truth in government by the best for the others? If that isn't good what is?

If it's not true that one man's more fitted by nature and training to manage difficult political affairs than another, nothing's true. And it's true that he can do it best without a mass of ignorant, uninstructed, sentimental people for ever jerking at the reins. Put the best on top—that's the gist of Toryism." Datcherd was looking at him cynically.

"And yet—you belong to the Young Liberals' League."

"Of course I do. Do you want me to enlarge on the gist and the beauties of Liberalism too? I could, only I won't, because you've just done so yourself. All that you've said about its making for freedom and enlightenment is profoundly true, and is why I am a Liberal. I insist on my right to be both. I am both. I hope I shall always be both."

Datcherd said, after a thoughtful moment, "I wish we had had this conversation three months ago. We didn't; I was reckless and hasty, and so we've made this mess of things."

"*Is* it a mess?" asked Eddy. "I'm sorry if so. It hasn't struck me in that light all this time."

"Don't think me ungrateful, Oliver," said Datcherd, quickly. "I'm not. Looking at things as you do, I suppose it was natural that you should have done as you have. Perhaps you might have let me a little more into your views beforehand than you did—but never mind that now. The fact that matters is that I find the Club in a state of mental confusion that I never expected, and it will take some time to settle it again, if we ever do. We want, as you know, to make the Club the nucleus of a sound Radical constituency. Well, upon my word, if there was an election now, I couldn't say which way some of them would vote. You may answer that it doesn't matter, as so few are voters yet; but it does. It's what I call a mess; and a silly mess, too. They've been playing the fool with things they ought to be keen enough about to take in deadly earnest. That's your doing. You seem to have become pretty popular, I must say; which is just the mischief of it. All I can do now is to try and straighten things out by degrees."

"You'd rather I didn't come and help any more, I suppose," said Eddy.

"To be quite frank, I would. In fact, I wouldn't have you at any price. You don't mind my speaking plainly? The mistake's been mine; but it *has* been a pretty idiotic mistake, and we mustn't have any more of it.... I ought never to have gone away. I shan't again, whatever any fools of doctors say."

Eddy held out his hand. "Goodbye. I'm really very sorry, Datcherd. I suppose I ought to have guessed what you would feel about all this."

"Honestly, I think you ought. But thank you very much, all the same, for all the trouble you've taken.... You're doing some reviewing work now, aren't you?" His tone implied that Eddy had better go on doing reviewing work, and desist from doing anything else.

Eddy left the house. He was sorry, and rather angry, and badly disappointed. He had been keen on the Club; he had hoped to go on helping with it. It seemed that he was not considered fit by anyone to have anything to do with clubs and such philanthropic enterprises. First the Vicar of St. Gregory's had turned him out because he had too many interests besides (Datcherd being one), and now Datcherd turned him out because he had tried to give the Club too many interests (the cause the vicar stood for being one). Nowhere did he seem to be wanted. He was a failure and an outcast. Besides which, Datcherd thought he had behaved dishonourably. Perhaps he had. Here he saw Datcherd's point of view. Even his friend the Ulsterman had obviously had the same thought about that. Eddy ruefully admitted that he had been an idiot not to know just how Datcherd would feel. But he was angry with Datcherd for feeling like that. Datcherd was narrow, opinionated, and unfair. So many people are, in an unfair world.

He went home and told Arnold, who said, "Of course. I can't think why you didn't know how it would be. I always told you you were being absurd, with your Blue Water lunatics, and your Food Tax ante-diluvians, and your conscription captains. (No, don't tell me about it's not being conscription; now is not the moment. You are down, and it is for me to talk.) You had better try your hand at no more good works, but stick to earning an honest livelihood, as long as they will give you any money for what you do. I daresay from a rumour I heard from Innes to-day, that it won't be long. I believe the *Daily Post* are contemplating a reduction in their literary staff, and they will very probably begin with you, unless you learn to restrain your redundant appreciations a little. No paper could bear up under that weight of indiscriminate enthusiasm for long."

"Hulbert told me I was to criticize more severely," said Eddy. "So I try to now. It's difficult, when I like a thing, to be severe about it. I wonder if one ought."

But he was really wondering more what Eileen Le Moine thought and would say about his difference with Datcherd.

He didn't discover this for a week. He called at 3, Campden Hill Road, and found both its occupants out. They did not write, as he had half expected, to ask him to come again, or to meet them anywhere. At last he met Eileen alone, coming out of an exhibition of Max Beerbohm cartoons. He had been going in, but he turned back on seeing her. She looked somehow altered, and grave, and she was more beautiful even than he had known, but tired, and with shadowed eyes of fire and softness; to him she seemed, vaguely, less of a child, and more of a woman. Perhaps it was Greece.... Somehow Greece, and all the worlds old and new, and all the seas, seemed between them as she looked at him with hardening eyes. An observer would have said from that look that she didn't like him; yet she had always liked him a good deal. A capricious person she was; all her friends knew that.

He turned back from the entrance door to walk with her, though she said, "Aren't you going in?"

"No," he said. "I've seen them once already. I'd rather see you now, if you don't mind. I suppose you're going somewhere? You wouldn't come and have tea with me first?"

She hesitated a moment, as if wondering whether she would, then said, "No; I'm going to tea with Billy's grandmother; she wants to hear about Greece. Then Billy and I are taking Jane to the Academy, to broaden her mind. She's never seen it yet, and it's time her education was completed."

She said it coldly, even the little familiar mockery of Jane and the Academy, and Eddy knew that she was angry with him. That he did not like, and he said quickly, "May I go with you as far as Gordon Place?" (which was where Billy's grandmother lived), and she answered with childish sullenness, "If we're going the one way at the one time I suppose we will be together," and said no more till he broke the silence as they crossed Leicester Square in the sunshine with, "Please, is anything the matter, Eileen?"

She turned and looked at him, her face hard in the shadow of the sweeping hat-brim, and flung back ironically, "It is not. Of course not; how would it be?"

Eddy made a gesture of despair with his hands.

"You're angry too. I knew it. You're all angry, because I had Tariff Reformers and Orangemen to lecture to the Club."

"D'you tell me so?" She still spoke in uncomfortable irony. "I expect you hoped we would be grateful and delighted at being dragged back from Greece just when Hugh was beginning to be better, and to enjoy things, by a letter from that miserable Pollard all about the way you had the Club spoilt. Why, we hadn't been to Olympia yet. We were just going there when Hugh insisted on calling for letters at Athens and got this. Letters indeed! Bridget and I didn't ask were there any for us; but Hugh always will. And of course, when he'd read it nothing would hold him; he must tear off home by the next train and arrive in London three weeks sooner than we'd planned. Now why, if you felt you had to go to spoil Hugh's club, couldn't you have had Pollard strangled first, the way he wouldn't be writing letters?"

"I wish I had," said Eddy, with bitter fervour. "I was a fool."

"And worse than that, so you were," said Eileen, unsparingly. "You were unprincipled, and then so wanting foresight that you wrecked your own schemes. Three weeks more, and you might have had twenty-one more captains and clergymen and young men from Ulster to complete the education of Hugh's young Liberals. As it is, Hugh thinks you've not done them much harm, though you did your best, and he's slaving away to put sense into them again. The good of Greece is all gone from him already; worry was just what he wasn't to do, and you've made him do it. He's living already again at top speed, and over-working, and being sad because it's all in such a silly mess. Hugh cares for his work more than for anything in the world," her voice softened to the protective cadence familiar to Eddy, "and you've hurt him in it. No one should hurt Hugh in his work, even a little. Didn't you know that?"

She looked at him now with eyes less hostile but more sad, as if her thoughts had left him and wandered to some other application of this principle. Indeed, as she said it, it had the effect of a creed, a statement of a governing principle of life, that must somehow be preserved intact while all else broke.

"Could I have known it would have hurt him—a few lectures?" Eddy protested against the unfairness of it, losing his temper a little. "You all talk as if Datcherd was the mistress of a girls' school, who is expected to protect her pupils from the contamination of degrading influences and finds they have been reading Nietsche or *Tom Jones*."

It was a mistake to say that. He might have known it. Eileen flushed pink with a new rush of anger.

"Is that so? Is that the way we speak of Hugh? I'll tell him you said so. No, I wouldn't trouble his ears with anything so paltry. I wonder do you know the way he speaks of you? He thinks you must be weak in the head, and he makes excuses for you, so he does; he never says an unkind word against you, only how you ought to be locked up and not let loose like ordinary people, and how he ought to have known you were like that and explained to you in so many words beforehand the principles he wanted maintained. As if he hadn't been too ill to explain anything, and as if any baby wouldn't have known, and as if any honourable person wouldn't have taken particular care, just when he was ill and away, to run things just the way he would like. And after that you call him a girls' school mistress...."

"On the contrary," said Eddy, crossly, "I said he wasn't. You are horribly unfair. Is it any use continuing this conversation?"

"It is not. Nor any other."

So, in her excitement, she got into a bus that was not going to Billy's grandmother, and he swallowed his pride and told her so, but she would not swallow hers and listen to him, but climbed on to the top, and was carried down Piccadilly, and would have to change at Hyde Park Corner.

Eileen was singularly poor at buses, Eddy reflected bitterly. He walked down to the Embankment, too crushed and unhappy to go home and risk meeting Arnold. He had been rude and ill-tempered to Eileen, and sneered at Datcherd to her, and she had been rude and ill-tempered to him, and would never forgive him, because it had been about Datcherd, her friend, loyalty to whom was the mainspring of her life. All her other friends might go by the board, if Datcherd but prospered. How much she cared, Eddy reflected, his anger fast fading into a pity and regret that hurt. For all her bitter words to him had that basis—a poignant caring for Datcherd, with his wrecked health, and his wrecked home, and his hopeless, unsatisfied love for her—a love which would never be satisfied, because he had principles which forbade it, and she had a love for him which would always preserve his principles and his life's work intact. And they were growing to care so much—Eddy had seen that in Eileen's face when first he met her at the Leicester Galleries—with such intensity, such absorbing flame, that it hurt and burnt.... Eddy did not want to watch it.

But one thing it had done for him; it had killed in him the last vestiges of that absurd emotion he had had for her, an emotion which had always been so hopeless, and for that very reason had never become, and never would become, love.

But he wanted to be friends. However much she had been the aggressor in the quarrel, however unfair, and unjust, and unkind she had been, still he was minded to write and say he was sorry, and would she please come to lunch and go on being friends.

He turned into Soho Square, and went back to his rooms. There he found a letter from his editor telling him that his services on the *Daily Post* would not be required after the end of May. It was not unexpected. The *Post* was economising in its literary staff, and starting on him. It was very natural, even inevitable, that they should; for his reviewing lacked discrimination, and his interest in the Club had often made him careless about his own job. He threw the letter at Arnold, who had just come in.

Arnold said, "I feared as much."

"What now, I wonder?" said Eddy, not caring particularly.

Arnold looked at him thoughtfully.

"Really, it's very difficult. I don't know.... You do so muddle things up, don't you? I wish you'd learn to do only one job at once and stick to it."

Eddy said bitterly, "It won't stick to me, unfortunately."

Arnold said, "If Uncle Wilfred would have you, would you come to us?"

Eddy supposed he would. Only probably Uncle Wilfred wouldn't have him. Later in the evening he got a telegram to say that his father had had a stroke, and could he come home at once. He caught a train at half-past eight, and was at Welchester by ten.

CHAPTER XI.

THE COUNTRY.

THE Dean was paralysed up the right side, his wife agitated and anxious, his daughter cross.

"It's absurd," said Daphne to Eddy, the morning after his arrival. "Father's no more sense than a baby. He insists on bothering about some article he hasn't finished for the *Church Quarterly* on the Synoptic Problem. As if one more like that mattered! The magazines are too full of them already."

But the Dean made it obvious to Eddy that it did matter, and induced him to find and decipher his rough notes for the end of the article, and write them out in proper form. He was so much better after an afternoon of that that the doctor said to Eddy, "How long can you stop at home?"

"As long as I can be any use. I have just given up one job and haven't begun another yet, so at present I am free."

"The longer you stay the better, both for your father and your mother," the doctor said. "You can take a lot of strain off Mrs. Oliver. Miss Daphne's very young—too young for much sick-nursing, I fancy; and the nurse can only do what nurses can do. He wants companionship, and someone who can do for him the sort of job you've been doing to-day."

So Eddy wrote to Arnold that he didn't know when he would be coming back to London. Arnold replied that whenever he did he could come into his uncle's publishing house. He added in a postscript that he had met Eileen and Datcherd at the Moulin d'Or, and Eileen had said, "Give Eddy my love, and say I'm sorry. Don't forget." Sorry about his father, Arnold understood, of course; but Eddy believed that more was meant by it than that, and that Eileen was throwing him across space her characteristically sweet and casual amends for her bitter words.

He went on with the Synoptic Problem. The Dean's notes were lucid and coherent, like all his work. It seemed to Eddy an interesting article, and the Dean smiled faintly when he said so. Eddy was appreciative and intelligent, if not learned or profound. The Dean had been afraid for a time that he was going to turn into a cleric of that active sort which is so absorbed in practical energies that it does not give due value to thoughtful theology. The Dean had reason to fear that too many High Church clergy were like this. But he had hopes now that Eddy, if in the end he did take Orders, might be of those who think out the faith that is in them, and tackle the problem of the Fourth Gospel. Perhaps he had had to, while managing Datcherd's free-thinking club.

"Are you still helping Datcherd?" the Dean asked, in the slow, hindered speech that was all he could use now.

"No. Datcherd has done with me. I managed things badly there, from his point of view. I wasn't exclusive enough for him," and Eddy, to amuse his father, told the story of that fiasco.

Daphne said, "Serve you right for getting an anti-suffragist to speak. How could you? They're always so deadly silly, and so dull. Worse, almost, than the other side, though that's saying a lot. I do think, Tedders, you deserved to be chucked out."

Daphne had blossomed into a militant. Mrs. Oliver had been telling Eddy about that the day before. Mrs. Oliver herself belonged to the respectable National Union for Women's Suffrage, the pure and reformed branch of it in Welchester established, non-militant, non-party, non-exciting. Daphne, and a few other bright and ardent young spirits, had joined the W.S.P.U., and had been endeavouring to militate in Welchester. Daphne had dropped some Jeye's disinfectant fluid, which is sticky and brown, into the pillar-box at the corner of the Close, and made disagreeable thereby a letter to herself from a neighbour asking her to tennis, and a letter to the Dean from a canon fixing the date (which was indecipherable) of a committee meeting.

Daphne looked critically at breakfast next day at these two results of her tactics, and called them "Jolly fine."

"Disgusting," said the Dean. "I didn't know we had these wild women in Welchester. Who on earth can it have been?"

"Me," said Daphne. "Alone I did it."

Scene: the Dean horrified, stern, and ashamed; Mrs. Oliver shocked and repressive; Daphne sulky and defiant, and refusing to promise not to do it again.

"We've joined the militants, several of us," she said.

"Who?" inquired her mother. "I'm sure Molly hasn't."

"No, Molly hasn't," said Daphne, with disgust. "All the Bellairs' are too frightfully well-bred to fight for what they ought to have. They're antis, all of them. Nevill approves of forcible feeding."

"So does anyone, of course," said the Dean. "Prisoners can't be allowed to die on our hands just because they are criminally insane. Once for all, Daphne, I will not have a repetition of this disgusting episode. Other people's daughters can make fools of themselves if they like, but mine isn't going to. Is that quite clear?"

Daphne muttered something and looked rebellious; but the Dean did not think she would flatly disobey him. She did not, in fact, repeat the disgusting episode of the Jeye, but she was found a few evenings later trying to set fire to a workmen's shelter after dark, and arrested. She was naturally anxious to go to prison, to complete her experiences, but she was given the option of a fine (which the Dean insisted, in spite of her protests, on paying), and bound over not to do it again. The Dean said after that that he was ashamed to look his neighbours in the face, and very shortly he had a stroke. Daphne decided reluctantly that militant methods must be in abeyance till he was recovered, and more fit to face shocks. To relieve herself, she engaged in a violent quarrel with Nevill Bellairs, who was home for Whitsuntide and ventured to remonstrate with her on her proceedings. They parted in sorrow and anger, and Daphne came home very cross, and abused Nevill to Eddy as a stick-in-the-mud.

"But it *is* silly to burn and spoil things," said Eddy. "Very few things are silly, I think, but that is, because it's not the way to get anything. You're merely putting things back; you're reactionaries. All the sane suffragists hate you, you know."

Daphne was not roused to say anything about peaceful methods having failed, and the time having come for violence, or any of the other things that are natural and usual to say in the circumstances; she was sullenly silent, and Eddy, glancing at her in surprise, saw her sombre and angry.

Wondering a little, he put it down to her disagreement with Nevill. Perhaps she really felt that badly. Certainly she and Nevill had been great friends during the last year. It was a pity they should quarrel over a difference of opinion; anything in the world, to Eddy, seemed a more reasonable cause of alienation. He looked at his young sister with a new respect, however; after all, it was rather respectable to care as much as that for a point of view.

Molly Bellairs threw more light on the business next day when Eddy went to tennis there (Daphne had refused to go).

"Poor Daffy," Molly said to Eddy when they were sitting out. "She's frightfully cross with Nevill for being anti-suffragist, and telling her she's silly to militate. And he's cross with her. She told him, I believe, that she wasn't going to be friends with him any more till he changed. And he never does change about anything, and she doesn't either, so there they are. It's *such* a pity, because they're really so awfully fond of each other. Nevill's miserable. Look at him."

Eddy looked, and saw Nevill, morose and graceful in flannels, smashing double faults into the net.

"He always does that when he's out of temper," Molly explained.

"Why does he care so much?" Eddy asked, with brotherly curiosity. "Do you mean he's *really* fond of Daffy? Fonder, I mean, than the rest of you are?"

"Quite differently." Molly became motherly and wise. "Haven't you seen it? It's been coming on for quite a year. *I* believe, Eddy, they'd be *engaged* by now if it wasn't for this."

"Oh, would they?" Eddy was interested. "But would they be such donkeys as to let this get in the way, if they want to be engaged? I thought Daffy had more sense."

Molly shook her head. "They think each other so wrong, you see, and they've got cross about it.... Well, I don't know. I suppose they're right, if they really do feel it's a question of right and wrong. You can't go on being friends with a person, let alone get engaged to them, if you feel they're behaving frightfully wrongly. You see, Daffy thinks it immoral of Nevill to be on the anti side in Parliament, and to approve of what she calls organised bullying, and he thinks it immoral of her to be a militant. *I* think Daffy's wrong, of course, but I can quite see that she couldn't get engaged to Nevill feeling as she does."

"Why," Eddy pondered, "can't they each see the other's point of view,—the good in it, not the bad? It's so absurd to quarrel about the respective merits of different principles, when all are so excellent."

"They're not," said Molly, rather sharply. "That's so like you, Eddy, and it's nonsense. What else should one quarrel about? What *I* think is absurd is to quarrel about personal things, like some people do."

"It's absurd to quarrel at all," said Eddy, and there they left it, and went to play tennis.

Before he went home, Colonel Bellairs proposed a scheme to him. His youngest boy, Bob, having been ill, had been ordered to spend the summer at home, and was not to go back to Eton till September. Meanwhile he wanted to keep up with his work, and they had been looking out for a tutor for him, some intelligent young public-school man who would know what he ought to be learning. As Eddy intended to be at home for the present, would he take up this job? The Colonel proposed a generous payment, and Eddy thought it an excellent plan. He went home engaged for the job, and started it next morning. Bob, who was sixteen, was, like all the Bellairs', neither clever nor stupid; his gifts were practical rather than literary, but he had a fairly serviceable head. Eddy found that he rather liked teaching. He had a certain power of transmitting his own interest in things to other people that was useful.

As the Dean got better, Eddy sometimes stayed on at the Hall after work hours, and played tennis or bumble-puppy with Molly and Bob before lunch, or helped Molly to feed the rabbits, or wash one of the dogs. There was a pleasant coherence and unity about these occupations, and about Molly and Bob, which Eddy liked. Meanwhile he acted as amanuensis and secretary to his father, and was useful and agreeable in the home.

Coherence and unity; these qualities seemed in the main sadly lacking in Welchester, as in other places. It was—country life is, life in Cathedral or any other cities is—a chaos of warring elements, disturbing to the onlooker. There are no communities now, village or other. In Welchester, and in the country round about it, there was the continuous strain of opposing interests. You saw it on the main road into Welchester, where villas and villa people ousted cottages and small farmers; ousted them, and made a different demand on life, set up a different, opposing standard. Then, in the heart of the town, was the Cathedral, standing on a hill and for a set of interests quite different again, and round about it were the canons' houses of old brick, and the Deanery, and they were imposing on life standards of a certain dignity and beauty and tradition and order, not in the least accepted either by the slum-yards behind Church Street, or by Beulah, the smug tabernacle just outside the Close. And the Cathedral society, the canons and their families, the lawyers, doctors, and unemployed gentry, kept themselves apart with satisfied gentility from the townspeople, the keepers of shops, the dentists, the auctioneers. Sentiment and opinion in Welchester was, in short, disintegrated, rent, at odds within itself. It returned a Conservative member, but only by a small majority; the large minority held itself neglected, unrepresented.

Out in the rolling green country beyond the town gates, the same unwholesome strife saddened field and lane and park. Land-owners, great and small, fought to the last ditch, the last ungenerous notice-board, with land-traversers; squires and keepers disagreed bitterly with poachers; tenant farmers saw life from an opposite angle to that of labourers; the parson differed from the minister, and often, alas, from his flock. It was as if all these warring elements, which might, from a common vantage-ground, have together conducted the exploration into the promised land, were staying at home disputing with one another as to the nature of that land. Some good, some better state of things, was in most of their minds to seek; but their paths of approach, all divergent, seemed to run weakly into waste places for want of a common energy. It was a saddening sight. The great heterogeneous unity conceived by civilised idealists seemed inaccessibly remote.

Eddy this summer took to writing articles for the *Vineyard* about the breaches in country life and how to heal them. The breach, for instance, between tenant-farmer and labourer; that was much on his mind. But, when he had written and written, and suggested and suggested, like many before him and since, the breach was no nearer being healed. He formed in his mind at this time a scheme for a new paper which he would like to start some day if anyone would back it, and if Denison's firm would publish it. And, after all, so many new papers are backed, but how inadequately, and started, and published, and flash like meteors across the sky, and plunge fizzling into the sea of oblivion to perish miserably—so why not this? He thought he would like it to be called *Unity*, and to have that for its glorious aim. All papers have aims beforehand (one may find them set forth in many a prospectus); how soon, alas, in many cases to be disregarded or abandoned in response to the exigencies of circumstance and demand. But the aim of *Unity* should persist, and, if heaven was kind, reach its mark.

Pondering on this scheme, Eddy could watch chaos with more tolerant eyes, since nothing is so intolerable if one is thinking of doing something, even a very little, to try and alleviate it. He carried on a correspondence with Arnold about it. Arnold said he didn't for a moment suppose his Uncle Wilfred would be so misguided as to have anything to do with such a scheme, but he might, of course. The great dodge with a new paper, was, Arnold said, the co-operative system; you collect a staff of eager contributors who will undertake to write for so many months without pay, and not want to get their own back again till after the thing is coining money, and then they share what profits there are, if any. If they could collect a few useful people for this purpose, such as Billy Raymond, and Datcherd, and Cecil Le Moine (only probably Cecil was too selfish), and John Henderson, and Margaret Clinton (a novelist friend of Arnold's), and various other intelligent men and women, the thing might be worked. And Bob Traherne and Dean Oliver, to represent two different Church standpoints, Eddy added to the list, and a field labourer he knew who would talk about small holdings, and a Conservative or two (Conservatives were conspicuously lacking in Arnold's list). Encouraged by Arnold's reception of the idea, Eddy replied by sketching his scheme for *Unity* more elaborately. Arnold answered, "If we get all or any of the people we've thought of to write for it, *Unity* will go its own way, regardless of schemes beforehand.... Have your Tories and parsons in if you must, only don't be surprised if they sink it.... The chief thing to mind about with a writer is, has he anything new to say? I hate all that sentimental taking up and patting on the back of ploughmen and navvies and tramps merely as such; it's silly, inverted snobbery. It doesn't follow that a man has anything to say that's worth hearing merely because he says it ungrammatically. Get day labourers to write about land-tenure if they have anything to say about it that's more enlightening than what you or I would say; but not unless; because they won't put it so well, by a long way. If ever I have anything to do with a paper, I shall see that it avoids sentimentality so far as is consistent with just enough popularity to live by."

It was still all in the air, of course, but Eddy felt cheered by the definite treatment Arnold was giving to his idea.

About the middle of June Arnold wrote that Datcherd had hopelessly broken down at last, and there seemed no chance for him, and he had given up everything and gone down to a cottage in Devonshire, probably to die there.

"Eileen has gone with him," Arnold added, in graver vein than usual. "I suppose she wants to look after him, and they both want not to waste the time that's left.... Of course, many people will be horrified, and think the worst. Personally, I think it a pity she should do it, because it means, for her, giving up a great deal, now and afterwards, though for him nothing now but a principle. The breaking of the principle is surprising in him, and really, if one comes to think of it, pretty sad, and a sign of how he's broken up altogether. Because he has always held these things uncivilised and wrong, and said so. I suppose he's too weak in body to say so any more, or to stand against his need and hers any longer. I think it a bad mistake, and I wish they wouldn't do it. Besides, she's too fine, and has too much to give, to throw it all at one dying man, as she's doing. What's it been in Datcherd all along that's so held her—he so sickly and wrecked and morose, she so brilliant and alive and young and full of genius and joy? Of course he's brilliant too, in his own way, and lovable, and interesting; but a failure for all that, and an unhappy failure, and now at the last a failure even as to his own principles of life. I suppose it has been always just that that has held her; his failure and need. These things are dark; but anyhow there it is; one never saw two people care for each other more or need each other more.... She was afraid of hurting his work by coming to him before; but the time for thinking of that is past, and I suppose she will stay with him now till the end, and it will be their one happy time. You know I think these things mostly a mistake, and these absorbing emotions uncivilised, and nearly all alliances ill-assorted, and this one will be condemned. But much she'll care for that when it is all over and he has gone. What will happen to her then I can't guess; she won't care much for anything any of us can do to help, for a long time. It is a pity. But such is life, a series of futile wreckages." He went on to other topics. Eddy didn't read the rest just then, but went out for a long and violent walk across country with his incredibly mongrel dog.

Confusion, with its many faces, its shouting of innumerable voices, overlay the green June country. For him in that hour the voice of pity and love rose dominant, drowning the other voices, that questioned and wondered and denied, as the cuckoos from every tree questioned and commented on life in their strange, late note. Love and pity; pity and love; mightn't these two resolve all discord at last? Arnold's point of view, that of the civilised person of sense, he saw and shared; Eileen's and Datcherd's he saw and felt; his own mother's, and the Bellairs', and that of those like-minded with them, he saw and appreciated; all were surely right, yet they did not make for harmony.

Meanwhile, a background to discord, the woods were green and the hedges starred pink with wild roses and the cow-parsley a white foam in the ditches, and the clouds shreds of white fleece in the blue above, and cows knee-deep in cool pools beneath spreading trees, and, behind the jubilance of larks and the other jocund little fowls, cried the perpetual questioning of the unanswered grey bird....

In the course of July, Eddy became engaged to Molly Bellairs, an event which, with all its preliminary and attendant circumstances, requires and will receive little treatment here. Proposals and their attendant emotions, though more interesting even than most things to those principally concerned, are doubtless so familiar to all as to be readily imagined, and can occupy no place in these pages. The fact emerges that Eddy and Molly, after the usual preliminaries, *did* become engaged. It must not be surmised that their emotions, because passed lightly over, were not of the customary and suitable fervour; in point of fact, both were very much in love. Both their families were pleased. The marriage, of course, was not to occur till Eddy was settled definitely into a promising profession, but that he hoped to be in the autumn, if he entered the Denisons' publishing firm and at the same time practised journalism.

"You should get settled with something permanent, my boy," said the Dean, who was by now well enough to talk like that. "I don't like this taking things up and dropping them."

"They drop me," Eddy explained, much as he had to Arnold once, but the Dean did not like him to put it like that, as anyone would rather his son dropped than was dropped.

"You know you can do well if you like," he said, being fairly started in that vein. "You did well at school and Cambridge, and you can do well now. And now that you're going to be married, you must give up feeling your way and occupying yourself with jobs that aren't your regular career, and get your teeth into something definite. It wouldn't be fair to Molly to play about with odd jobs, even useful and valuable ones, as you have been doing. You wouldn't think of schoolmastering at all, I suppose? With your degree you could easily get a good place." The Dean hankered after a scholastic career for his son; besides, schoolmasters so often end in Orders. But Eddy said he thought he would prefer publishing or journalism, though it didn't pay so well at first. He told the Dean about the proposed paper and the co-operative system, which was sure to work so well.

The Dean said, "I haven't any faith in all these new papers, whatever the system. Even the best die. Look at the *Pilot*. And the *Tribune*."

Eddy looked back across the ages at the *Pilot* and the *Tribune*, whose deaths he just remembered.

"There've been plenty died since those," he remarked. "Those whom the gods love, etcetera. But lots have lived, too. If you come to that, look at the *Times*, the *Spectator*, and the *Daily Mirror*. They were new once. So was the *English Review*; so was *Poetry and Drama*; so was the *New Statesman*; so was the *Blue Review*. They're alive yet. Then why not *Unity*? Even if it has a short life, it may be a merry one."

"To heal divisions," mused the Dean. "A good aim, of course. Though probably a hopeless one. One makes it one's task, you know, to throw bridges, as far as one can, between the Church and the agnostics, and the Church and dissent. And lock at the result. A friendly act of conciliation on the part of one of our bishops calls forth torrents of bitter abuse in the columns of our Church papers. The High Church party is so unmanageable: it's stiff: it stands out for differences: it won't be brought in. How can we ever progress towards unity if the extreme left remains in that state of wilful obscurantism and unchristian intolerance?... Of course, mind, there are limits; one would fight very strongly against disestablishment or disendowment; but the ritualists seem to be out for quarrels over trifles." He added, because Eddy had worked in St. Gregory's, "Of course, individually, there are numberless excellent High Churchmen; one doesn't want to run down their work. But they'll never stand for unity."

"Quite," said Eddy, meditating on unity. "That's exactly what Finch and the rest say about the Broad Church party, you know. And it's what dissenters say about Church people, and Church people about dissenters. The fact is, so few parties do stand for unity. They nearly all stand for faction."

"I don't think we Broad Churchmen stand for faction," said the Dean, and Eddy replied that nor did the High Churchmen think they did, nor dissenters either. They all thought they were aiming at unity, but it was the sort of unity attained by the survivor of the *Nancy* brig, or the tiger of Riga, that was the ideal of most parties; it was doubtless also the ideal of a boa-constrictor. Mrs. Oliver, who had come into the room and wasn't sure it was in good taste to introduce light verse and boa-constrictors into religious discussions, said, "You seem to be talking a great deal of nonsense, dear boy. Everard, have you had your drops yet?"

In such fruitful family discourse they wiled away the Dean's convalescence.

Meanwhile Molly, jolly and young and alive, with her brown hair curling in the sun, and her happy infectious laugh and her bright, eager, amber eyes full of friendly mirth, was a sheer joy. If she too "stood for" anything beyond herself, it was for youth and mirth and jollity and country life in the open; all sweet things. Eddy and she liked each other rather more each day. They made a plan for Molly to spend a month or so in the autumn with her aunt that lived in Hyde Park Terrace, so that she and Eddy should be near each other.

"They're darlings," said Molly, of her uncle and aunt and cousins. "So jolly and hospitable. You'll love them."

"I'm sure I shall. And will they love me?" inquired Eddy, for this seemed even more important.

Molly said of course they would.

"Do they love most people?" Eddy pursued his investigations.

Molly considered that. "Well ... most ... that's a lot, isn't it. No, Aunt Vyvian doesn't do that, I should think. Uncle Jimmy more. He's a sailor, you know; a captain, retired. He seems awfully young, always; much younger than me.... One thing about Aunt Vyvian is, I should think you'd know it pretty quick if she didn't like you."

"She'd say so, would she?"

"She'd snub you. She's rather snippy sometimes, even to me and people she's fond of. Only one gets used to it, and it doesn't mean anything except that she likes to amuse herself. But she's frightfully particular, and if she didn't like you she wouldn't have anything to do with you."

"I see. Then it's most important that she should. What can I do about it?"

"Oh, just be pleasant, and make yourself as entertaining as you can, and pretend to be fairly sensible and intelligent.... She wouldn't like it if she thought you were, well, a socialist, or an anarchist, or a person who was trying to do something and couldn't, like people who try and get plays taken; or if I was a suffragette. She thinks people *oughtn't* to be like that, because they don't get on. And, too, she likes very much to be amused. *You'll* be all right, of course."

"Sure to be. I'm such a worldly success. Well, I shall haunt her doorstep whether she likes me or not."

"If she dared not to," said Molly indignantly, "I should walk straight out of her house and never go into it again, and make Nevill take me into his rooms instead. I should jolly well think she *would* like you!"

CHAPTER XII.

HYDE PARK TERRACE.

FORTUNATELY Mrs. Crawford did like Eddy (he presumed, therefore, that she did not know he was a socialist and a suffragist, and had tried to do many things he couldn't), so Molly did not have to walk out of the house. He liked her too, and went to her house very frequently. She was pretty and clever and frankly worldly, and had a sweet trailing voice, a graceful figure, and two daughters just out, one of whom was engaged already to a young man in the Foreign Office.

She told Molly, "I like your young man, dear; he has pleasant manners, and seems to appreciate me," and asked him to come to the house as often as he could. Eddy did so. He came to lunch and dinner, and met pleasant, polite, well-dressed people. (You had to be rather well-dressed at the Crawfords': they expected it, as so many others do, with what varying degrees of fulfilment!) It is, of course, as may before have been remarked in these pages, exceedingly important to dress well. Eddy knew this, having been well brought up, and did dress as well as accorded with his station and his duties. He quite saw the beauty of the idea, as of the other ideas presented to him. He also, however, saw the merits of the opposite idea held by some of his friends, that clothes are things not worth time, money, or trouble, and fashion an irrelevant absurdity. He always assented sincerely to Arnold when he delivered himself on this subject, and with equal sincerity to the tacit recognition of high standards that he met at the Crawfords' and elsewhere.

He also met at the Crawfords' their nephew Nevill Bellairs, who was now parliamentary secretary to an eminent member, and more than ever admirable in his certainty about what was right and what wrong. The Crawfords too were certain about that. To hear Nevill on Why Women should Not Vote was to feel that he and Daphne must be for ever sundered, and, in fact, were best apart. Eddy came to that melancholy conclusion, though he divined that their mutual and unhappy love still flourished.

"You're unfashionable, Nevill," his aunt admonished him. "You should try and not be that more than you can help."

Captain Crawford, a simple, engaging, and extraordinarily youthful sailor man of forty-six, said, "Don't be brow-beaten, Nevill; I'm with you," for that was the sort of man he was; and the young man from the Foreign Office said how a little while ago he had approved of a limited women's suffrage, but since the militants, etc., etc., and everyone he knew was saying the same.

"I am sure they are," Mrs. Crawford murmured to Eddy. "What a pity it does not seem to him a sufficient reason for abstaining from the remark himself. I do so dislike the subject of the suffrage; it makes everyone so exceedingly banal and obvious. I never make any remarks about it myself, for I have a deep fear that if I did so they might not be more original than that."

"Mine certainly wouldn't," Eddy agreed. "Militant suffragism is like the weather, a safety-valve for all our worst commonplaces. Only it's unlike the weather in being a little dull in itself, whereas the weather is an agitatingly interesting subject, as a rule inadequately handled.... You know, I've no objection to commonplace remarks myself, I rather like them. That's why I make them so often, I suppose."

"I think you have no objection to any kind of remarks," Mrs. Crawford commented. "You are fortunate."

Nevill said from across the room, "How's the paper getting on, Eddy? Is the first number launched yet?"

"Not yet. Only the dummy. I have a copy of the dummy here; look at it. We have filled it with the opinions of eminent persons on the great need that exists for our paper. We wrote to many. Some didn't answer. I suppose they were not aware of this great need, which is recognised so clearly by others. The strange thing is that *Unity* has never been started before, considering how badly it is obviously wanted. We have here encouraging words from politicians, authors, philanthropists, a bishop, an eminent rationalist, a fellow of All Souls, a landlord, a labour member, and many others. The bishop says, 'I am greatly interested in the prospectus you have sent me of your proposed new paper. Without committing myself to agreement with every detail, I may say that the lines on which it is proposed to conduct *Unity* promise a very useful and attractive paper, and one which should meet a genuine need and touch an extensive circle.' The labour member says, 'Your new paper is much needed, and with such fine ideals should be of great service to all.' The landlord says, 'Your articles dealing with country matters should meet a long-felt demand, and make for good feeling between landlords, tenants and labourers.' The rationalist says, 'Precisely what we want.' The Liberal politician says, 'I heartily wish all success to *Unity*. A good new paper on those lines cannot fail to be of inestimable service.' The Unionist says, 'A capital paper, with excellent ideals.' The philanthropist says, 'I hope it will wage relentless war against the miserable internal squabbles which retard our social efforts.' Here's a more tepid one—he's an author. He only says, 'There may be scope for such a paper, amid the ever-increasing throng of new journalistic enterprises. Anyhow there is no harm in trying.' A little damping, he was. Denison was against putting it in, but I think it so rude, when you've asked a man for a word of encouragement, and he gives it you according to his means, not to use it. Of course we had to draw the line somewhere. Shore merely said, 'It's a free country. You can hang yourselves if you like.' We didn't put in that. But on the whole people are obviously pining for the paper, aren't they. Of course they all think we're going to support their particular pet party and project. And so we are. That is why I think we shall sell so well—touch so extensive a circle, as the bishop puts it."

"As long as you help to knock another plank from beneath the feet of this beggarly government, I'll back you through thick and thin," said Captain Crawford.

"Are you going on the Down-with-the-Jews tack?" Nevill asked. "That's been overdone, I think; it's such beastly bad form."

"All the same," murmured Captain Crawford, "I don't care about the Hebrew."

"We're not," said Eddy, "going on a down-with-anybody tack. Our *métier* is to encourage the good, not to discourage anyone. That, as I remarked before, is why we shall sell so extremely well."

Mrs. Crawford said, "Humph. It sounds to me a trifle savourless. A little abuse hasn't usually been found, I believe, to reduce the sales of a paper appreciably. We most of us like to see our enemies hauled over the coals; or, failing our enemies, some innocuous and eminent member of an unpopular and over-intelligent race. In short, we like to see a fine hot quarrel going on. If *Unity* isn't going to quarrel with anyone, I shall certainly not subscribe."

"You shall have it gratis," said Eddy. "It is obviously, as the eminent rationalist puts it, precisely what you need."

Nevill said, "By the way, what's happening to that Radical paper of poor Hugh Datcherd's? Is it dead?"

"Yes. It couldn't have survived Datcherd; no one else could possibly take it on. Besides, he financed it entirely himself; it never anything near paid its way, of course. It's a pity; it was interesting."

"Like it's owner," Mrs. Crawford remarked. "He too, one gathers, was a pity, though no doubt an interesting one. The one failure in a distinguished family."

"I should call all the Datcherds a pity, if you ask me," said Nevill. "They're wrong-headed Radicals. All agnostics, too, and more or less anti-church."

"All the same," said his aunt, "they're not failures, mostly. They achieve success; even renown. They occasionally become cabinet ministers. I ask no more of a family than that. You may be as wrong-headed, radical, and anti-church as you please, Nevill, if you attain to being a cabinet minister. Of course they have disadvantages, such as England expecting them not to invest their money as they would prefer, and so on; but on the whole an enviable career. Better even than running a paper which meets a long-felt demand."

"But the paper's much more fun," Molly put in, and her aunt returned, "My dear child, we are not put into this troubled world to have fun, though I have noticed that you labour under that delusion."

The young man from the Foreign Office said, "It's not a delusion that can survive in my profession, anyhow. I must be getting back, I'm afraid," and they all went away to do something else. Eddy arranged to meet Molly and her aunt at tea-time, and take them to Jane Dawn's studio; he had asked her if he might bring them to see her drawings.

They met at Mrs. Crawford's club, and drove to Blackfriars' Road.

"*Where?*" inquired Mrs. Crawford, after Eddy's order to the driver.

"Pleasance Court, Blackfriars' Road," Eddy repeated.

"Oh! I somehow had an idea it was Chelsea. That's where one often finds studios; but, after all, there must be many others, if one comes to think of it."

"Perhaps Jane can't afford Chelsea. She's not poor, but she spends her money like a child. She takes after her father, who is extravagant, like so many professors."

"Chelsea's supposed to be cheap, my dear boy. That's why it's full of struggling young artists."

"I daresay Pleasance Court is cheaper. Besides, it's pleasant. They like it."

"They?"

"Jane and her friend Miss Peters, who shares rooms with her. Rather a jolly sort of girl; though——" On second thoughts Eddy refrained from mentioning that Sally Peters was a militant and had been in prison; he remembered that Mrs. Crawford found the subject tedious.

But militancy will out, as must have been noticed by many. Before the visitors had been there ten minutes, Sally referred to

the recent destruction of the property of a distinguished widowed
lady in such laudatory terms that Mrs. Crawford discerned her in
a minute, raised a disapproving lorgnette at her, murmured,
"They devour widows' houses, and for a pretence make long
speeches," and turned her back on her. Jolly sorts of girls who
were also criminal lunatics were not suffered in the sphere of her
acquaintance.

Jane's drawings were obviously charming; also they were the
drawings of an artist, not of a young lady of talent. Mrs.
Crawford, who knew the difference, perceived that, and gave
them the tribute she always ceded to success. She thought she
would ask Jane to lunch one day, without, of course, the blue-
eyed child who devoured widows' houses. She did so presently.

Jane said, "Thank you so much, but I'm afraid I can't," and
knitted her large forehead a little, in her apologetic way, so
obviously trying to think of a suitable reason why she couldn't,
that Mrs. Crawford came to her rescue with "Perhaps you're too
busy," which was gratefully accepted.

"I am rather busy just now." Jane was very polite, very
deprecating, but inwardly she reproached Eddy for letting in on
her strange ladies who asked her to lunch.

That no one ought to be too busy for social engagements, was
what Mrs. Crawford thought, and she turned a little crisper and
cooler in manner. Molly was standing before a small drawing in
a corner—a drawing of a girl, bare-legged, childish, half elfin,
lying among sedges by a stream, one leg up to the knee in water,
and one arm up to the elbow. Admirably the suggestion had been
caught of a small wild thing, a little half-sulky animal. Molly
laughed at it.

"That's Daffy, of course. It's not like her—and yet it *is* her. A
sort of inside look it's got of her; hasn't it, Eddy? I suppose it
looks different because Daffy's always so neat and tailor-made,
and never *would* be like that. It's a different Daffy, but it is
Daffy."

"Your pretty little sister, isn't it, Eddy," said Mrs. Crawford, who had met Daphne at Welchester. "Yes, that's clever. 'Undine,' you call it. Why? Has she no soul?"

Jane smiled and retired from this question. She seldom explained why her pictures were so called; they just were.

Molly was not looking at Undine. Her glance had fallen on a drawing near it. It was another drawing of a girl; a very beautiful girl, playing a violin. It was called "Life." No one would have asked why about this; the lightly poised figure, the glowing eyes under their shadowing black brows, the fiddle tucked away under the round chin, and the dimples tucked away in the round cheeks, the fine supple hands, expressed the very spirit of life, all its joy and brilliance and genius and fire, and all its potential tragedy. Molly looked at it without comment, as she might have looked at a picture of some friend of the artist's who had died a sad death. She knew that Eileen Le Moine had died, from her point of view; she knew that she had spent the last months of Hugh Datcherd's life with him, for Eddy had told her. She had said to Eddy that this was dreadful and wicked. Eddy had said, "They don't think it is, you see." Molly had said that what they thought made no difference to right and wrong; Eddy had replied that it made all the difference in the world. She had finally turned on him with, "But *you* think it dreadful, Eddy?" and he had, to her dismay, shaken his head.

"Not as they're doing it, I don't. It's all right. You'd know it was all right if you knew them, Molly. It's been, all along, the most faithful, loyal, fine, simple, sad thing in the world, their love. They've held out against it just so long as to give in would have hurt anyone but themselves; now it won't, and she's giving herself to him that he may die in peace. Don't judge them, Molly."

But she had judged them so uncompromisingly, so unyieldingly, that she had never referred to the subject again, for fear it should come between Eddy and her. A difference of principle was the one thing Molly could not bear. To her this thing, whatever its excuse, was wrong, against the laws of the Christian Church, in fine, wicked. And it was Eddy's friends who had done it, and he didn't want her to judge them; she must say nothing, therefore. Molly's ways were ways of peace.

Mrs. Crawford peered through her lorgnette at the drawing. "What's that delicious thing? 'Life.' Quite; just that. That is really utterly charming. Who's the original? Why, it's———" She stopped suddenly.

"It's Mrs. Le Moine, the violinist," said Jane.

"She's a great friend of ours," Sally interpolated, in childish pride, from behind. "I expect you've heard her play, haven't you?"

Mrs. Crawford had. She recognised the genius of the picture, which had so exquisitely caught and imprisoned the genius of the subject.

"Of course; who hasn't? A marvellous player. And a marvellous picture."

"It's Eileen all over," said Eddy, who knew it of old.

"Hugh bought it, you know," said Jane. "And when he died Eileen sent it back to me. I thought perhaps you and Eddy," she turned to Molly, "might care to have it for a wedding-present, with 'Undine.' "

Molly thanked her shyly, flushing a little. She would have preferred to refuse 'Life,' but her never-failing courtesy and tenderness for people's feelings drove her to smile and accept.

It was then that someone knocked on the studio door. Sally went to open it; cried, "Oh, Eileen," and drew her in, an arm about her waist.

She was not very like Jane's drawing of her just now. The tragic elements of Life had conquered and beaten down its brilliance and joy; the rounded white cheeks were thin, and showed, instead of dimples, the fine structure of the face and jaw; the great deep blue eyes brooded sombrely under sad brows; she drooped a little as she stood. It was as if something had been quenched in her, and left her as a dead fire. The old flashing smile had left only the wan, strange ghost of itself. If Jane had drawn her now, or any time since the middle of August, she would rather have called the drawing "Wreckage." To Eddy and all her friends she and her wrecked joy, her quenched vividness, stabbed at a pity beyond tears.

Molly looked at her for a moment, and turned rosy red all over her wholesome little tanned face, and bent over a picture near her.

Mrs. Crawford looked at her, through her, above her, and said to Jane, "Thank you so much for a delightful afternoon. We really must go now."

Jane said, slipping a hand into Eileen's, "Oh, but you'll have tea, won't you? I'm so sorry; we ought to have had it earlier.... Do you know Mrs. Le Moine? Mrs. Crawford; and *you* know each other, of course," she connected Eileen and Molly with a smile, and Molly put out a timid hand.

Mrs. Crawford's bow was so slight that it might have been not a bow at all. "Thank you, but I'm afraid we mustn't stop. We have enjoyed your delightful drawings exceedingly. Goodbye."

"Must you both go?" said Eddy to Molly. "Can't you stop and have tea and go home with me afterwards?"

"I'm afraid not," Molly murmured, still rosy.

"Are you coming with us, Eddy?" asked Molly's aunt, in her sweet, sub-acid voice. "No? Goodbye then. Oh, don't trouble, please, Miss Dawn; Eddy will show us out." Her faint bow comprehended the company.

Eddy came with them to their carriage.

"I'm sorry you won't stop," he said.

Mrs. Crawford's fine eyebrows rose a little.

"You could hardly expect me to stop, still less to let Molly stop, in company with a lady of Mrs. Le Moine's reputation. She has elected to become, as you of course are aware, one of the persons whose acquaintance must be dispensed with by all but the unfastidious. You are not going to dispense with it, I perceive? Very well; but you must allow Molly and me to take the ordinary course of the world in such matters. Goodbye."

Eddy, red as if her words had been a whip in his face, turned back into the house and shut the door rather violently behind him, as if by the gesture he would shut out all the harsh, coarse judgments of the undiscriminating world. He climbed the stairs to the studio, and found them having tea and discussing pictures, from their own several points of view, not the world's. It was a rest.

Mrs. Crawford, as they drove over the jolting surface of Blackfriars' Road, said, "Very odd friends your young man has, darling. And what a very unpleasant region they live in. It is just as well for the sake of the carriage wheels that we shall never have to go there again. We can't, of course, if we are liable to meet people of no reputation there. I'm sure you know nothing about things like that, but I'm sorry to say that Mrs. Le Moine has done things she ought not to have done. One may continue to admire her music, as one may admire the acting of those who lead such unfortunate lives on the stage; but one can't meet her. Eddy ought to know that. Of course it's different for him. Men may meet anyone; in fact, I believe they do; and no one thinks the worse of them. But I can't; still less, of course, you. I don't suppose your dear mother would like me to tell you about her, so I won't."

"I know," said Molly, blushing again and feeling she oughtn't to. "Eddy told me. He's a great friend of hers, you see."

"Oh, indeed. Well, girls know everything now-a-days, of course. In fact, everyone knows this; both she and Hugh Datcherd were such well-known people. I don't say it was so very dreadfully wrong, what they did; and of course Dorothy Datcherd left Hugh in the lurch first—but you wouldn't have heard of that, no—only it does put Mrs. Le Moine beyond the pale. And, in fact, it is dreadfully wrong to fly in the face of everybody's principles and social codes; of course it is."

Molly cared nothing for everyone's principles and social codes; but she knew it was dreadfully wrong, what they had done. She couldn't even reason it out; couldn't formulate the real reason why it was wrong; couldn't see that it was because it was giving rein to individual desire at the expense of the violation of a system which on the whole, however roughly and crudely, made for civilisation, virtue, and intellectual and moral progress; that it was, in short, a step backwards into savagery, a giving up of ground gained. Arnold Denison, more clear-sighted, saw that; Molly, with only her childlike, unphilosophical, but intensely vivid recognition of right and wrong to help her, merely knew it was wrong. From three widely different standpoints those three, Molly, Arnold Denison, Mrs. Crawford, joined in that recognition. Against them stood Eddy, who saw only the right in it, and the stabbing, wounding pity of it....

"It is extremely fortunate," said Mrs. Crawford, "that that young woman Miss Dawn refused to come to lunch. I daresay she knew she wasn't fit for lunch, with such people straying in and out of her rooms and she holding their hands. I give her credit so far. As for the plump fair child, she is obviously one of those vulgarians I insist on not hearing mentioned. Very strange friends, darling, your...."

"I'm sure nearly all Eddy's friends are very nice," Molly broke in. "Miss Dawn was staying at the Deanery at Christmas, you know. I'm sure she's nice, and she draws beautifully. And I expect Miss Peters is nice too; she's so friendly and jolly, and has such pretty hair and eyes. And...."

"You can stop there, dearest. If you are proceeding to say that you are sure Mrs. Le Moine is nice too, you can spare yourself the trouble."

"I wasn't," said Molly unhappily, and lifted her shamed, honest, amber eyes to her aunt's face. "Of course ... I know ... she can't be."

Her aunt gave her a soothing pat on the shoulder. "Very well, pet: don't worry about it. I'm afraid you will find that there are a large number of people in the world, and only too many of them aren't at all nice. Shockingly sad, of course; but if one took them all to heart one would sink into an early grave. The worst of this really is that we have lost our tea. We might drop in on the

Tommy Durnfords; it's their day, surely.... When shall you see Eddy next, by the way?"

"I think doesn't he come to dinner to-morrow?"

"So he does. Well, he and I must have a good talk."

Molly looked at her doubtfully. "Aunt Vyvian, I don't think so. Truly I don't."

"Well, I do, my dear. I'm responsible to your parents for you, and your young man's got to be careful of you, and I shall tell him so."

She told him so in the drawing-room after dinner next evening. She sat out from bridge on purpose to tell him. She said, "I was surprised and shocked yesterday afternoon, Eddy, as no doubt you gathered."

Eddy admitted that he had gathered that. "Do you mind if I say that I was too, a little?" he added. "Is that rude? I hope not."

"Not in the least. I've no doubt you were shocked; but I don't think really that you can have been much surprised, you know. Did you honestly expect me and Molly to stay and have tea with Mrs. Le Moine? She's not a person whom Molly ought to know. She's stepped deliberately outside the social pale, and must stay there. Seriously, Eddy, you mustn't bring her and Molly together."

"Seriously," said Eddy, "I mean to. I want Molly to know and care for all my friends. Of course she'll find in lots of them things she wouldn't agree with; but that's no barrier. I can't shut her out, don't you see? I know all these people so awfully well, and see so much of them; of course she must know them too. As for Mrs. Le Moine, she's one of the finest people I know; I should think anyone would be proud to know her. Surely one can't be rigid about things?"

"One can," Mrs. Crawford asserted. "One can, and one is. One draws one's line. Or rather the world draws it for one. Those who choose to step outside it must remain outside it."

Eddy said softly, "Bother the world!"

"I'm not going," she returned, "to do any such thing. I belong to the world, and am much attached to it. And about this sort of thing it happens to be entirely right. I abide by its decrees, and so must Molly, and so must you."

"I had hoped," he said, "that you, as well as Molly, would make friends with Eileen. She needs friendship rather. She's hurt and broken; you must have seen that yesterday."

"Indeed, I hardly looked. But I've no doubt she would be. I'm sorry for your unfortunate friend, Eddy, but I really can't know her. You didn't surely expect me to ask her here, to meet Chrissie and Dulcie and my innocent Jimmy, did you? What will you think of next? Well, well, I'm going to play bridge now, and you can go and talk to Molly. Only don't try and persuade her to meet your scandalous friends, because I shall not allow her to, and she has no desire to if I did. Molly, I am pleased to say, is a very right-minded and well-conducted girl."

Eddy discovered that this was so. Molly evinced no desire to meet Eileen Le Moine. She said "Aunt Vyvian doesn't want me to."

"But," Eddy expostulated, "she's constantly with the rest—Jane and Sally, and Denison, and Billy Raymond, and Cecil Le Moine, and all that set—you can't help meeting her sometimes."

"I needn't meet any of them much, really," said Molly.

Eddy disagreed. "Of course you need. They're some of my greatest friends. They've got to be your friends too. When we're married they'll come and see us constantly, I hope, and we shall go and see them. We shall always be meeting. I awfully want you to get to know them quickly. They're such good sorts, Molly; you'll like them all, and they'll love you."

There was an odd doubtful look in Molly's eyes.

"Eddy," she said after a moment, painfully blushing, "I'm awfully sorry, and it sounds priggish and silly—but I *can't* like people when I think they don't feel rightly about right and wrong. I suppose I'm made like that. I'm sorry."

"You precious infant." He smiled at her distressed face. "You're made as I prefer. But you see, they *do* feel rightly about things; they really do, Molly."

"Then," her shamed, averted eyes seemed to say, "why don't they act rightly?"

"Just try," he besought her, "to understand their points of view—everyone's point of view. Or rather, don't bother about points of view; just know the people, and you won't be able to help caring for them. People are like that—so much more alive and important than what they think or do, that none of that seems to matter. Oh, don't put up barriers, Molly. Do love my friends. I want you to. I'll love all yours; I will indeed, whatever dreadful things they've done or are doing. I'll love them even if they burn widows' houses, or paint problem pictures for the Academy, or write prize novels, or won't take in *Unity*. I'll love them through everything. Won't you love mine a little, too?"

She laughed back at him, unsteadily.

"Idiot, of course I will. I will indeed. I'll love them nearly all. Only I can't love things I hate, Eddy. Don't ask me to do that, because I can't."

"But you mustn't hate, Molly. Why hate? It isn't what things are there for, to be hated. Look here. Here are you and I set down in the middle of all this jolly, splendid, exciting jumble of things, just like a toy-shop, and we can go round looking at everything, touching everything, tasting everything (I used always to try to taste tarts and things in shops, didn't you?) Well isn't it all jolly and nice, and don't you like it? And here you sit and talk of hating!"

Molly was looking at him with her merry eyes unusually serious.

"But Eddy—you're just pretending when you talk of hating nothing. You know you hate some things yourself; there are some things everyone must hate. You know you do."

"Do I?" Eddy considered it. "Why, yes, I suppose so; some things. But very few."

"There's good," said Molly, with a gesture of one hand, "and there's bad...." she swept the other. "They're quite separate, and they're fighting."

Eddy observed that she was a Manichean Dualist.

"Don't know what that is. But it seems to mean an ordinary sensible person, so I hope I am. Aren't you?"

"I think not. Not to your extent, anyhow. But I quite see your point of view. Now will you see mine? And Eileen's? And all the others? Anyhow, will you think it over, so that by the time we're married you'll be ready to be friends?"

Molly shook her head.

"It's no use, Eddy. Don't let's talk about it any more. Come and play coon-can; I do like it such a lot better than bridge; it's so much sillier."

"I like them all," said Eddy.

CHAPTER XIII.

MOLLY.

EDDY next Sunday collected a party to row up to Kew. They were Jane Dawn, Bridget Hogan, Billy Raymond, Arnold Denison, Molly and himself, and they embarked in a boat at Crabtree Lane at two o'clock, and all took turns of rowing except Bridget, who, as has been observed before, was a lily of the field, and insisted on remaining so. She, Molly, and Eddy may be called the respectable-looking members of the party; Jane, Arnold, and Billy were sublimely untidy, which Eddy knew was a pity, because of Molly, who was always a daintily arrayed, fastidiously neat child. But it did not really matter. They were all very happy. The others made a pet and plaything of Molly, whose infectious, whole-hearted chuckle and naïve high spirits pleased them. She and Eddy decided to live in a river-side house, and made selections as they rowed by.

"You'd be better off in Soho," said Arnold.

"Eddy would be nearer his business, and nearer the shop we're going to start presently. Besides, it's more select. You can't avoid the respectable resident, up the river."

"The cheery non-resident, too, which is worse," added Miss Hogan. "Like us. The river on a holiday is unthinkable. We were on it all Good Friday last year, which seems silly, but I suppose we must have had some wise purpose. Why was it, Billy? Do you remember? You came, didn't you? And you, Jane. And Eileen and Cecil, I think. Anyhow never again. Oh yes, and we took some poor starved poet of Billy's—a most unfortunate creature, who proved, didn't he, to be unable even to write poetry. Or, indeed, to sit still in a boat. One or two very narrow shaves we had I remember. He's gone into Peter Robinson's since, I believe, as walker. So much nicer for him in every way. I saw him there last Tuesday. I gave him a friendly smile and asked how he was, but I think he had forgotten his past life, or else he had understood me to be asking the way to the stocking department, for he only replied, "Hose, madam?" Then I remembered that that was partly why he had failed to be a poet, because he would call stockings hose, and use similar unhealthy synonyms. So I concluded with pleasure that he had really found his vocation, the one career where such synonyms are suitable, and, in fact, necessary."

"He's a very nice person, Nichols," Billy said; "he still writes a little, but I don't think he'll ever get anything taken. He can't get rid of the idea that he's got to be elegant. It's a pity, because he's really got a little to say."

"Yes; quite a little, isn't it. Poor dear."

Eddy asked hopefully, "Would he do us an article for *Unity* from the shop walker's point of view, about shop life, and the relations between customers and shop people?"

Billy shook his head. "I'm sure he wouldn't. He'd want to write you a poem about something quite different instead. He hates the shop, and he won't write prose; he finds it too homely. And if he did, it would be horrible stuff, full of commencing, and hose, and words like that."

"And corsets, and the next pleasure, and kindly walk this way. It might be rather delightful really. I should try to get him to, Eddy."

"I think I will. We rather want the shopman's point of view, and it's not easy to get."

They were passing Chiswick Mall. Molly saw there the house she preferred.

"Look, Eddy. That one with wistaria over it, and the balcony. What's it called? The Osiers. What a nice name. Do let's stop and find out if we can have it."

"Well, someone obviously lives there; in fact, I see someone on the balcony. He might think it odd of us, do you think?"

"But perhaps he's leaving. Or perhaps he'd as soon live somewhere else, if we found a nice place for him. I wonder who it is?"

"I don't know. We might find out who his doctor is, and get him to tell him it's damp and unhealthy. It looks fairly old."

"And they say those osier beds are most unwholesome," Bridget added.

"It's heavenly. And look, there's a heron.... Can't we land on the island?"

"No. Bridget says it's unwholesome."

So they didn't, but went on to Kew. There they landed and went to look for the badger in the gardens. They did not find him. One never does. But they had tea. Then they rowed down again to Crabtree Lane, and their ways diverged.

Eddy went home with Molly. She said, "It's been lovely, Eddy," and he said "Hasn't it." He was pleased, because Molly and the others had got on so well and made such a happy party. He said, "When we're at the Osiers we'll often do that."

She said "Yes," thoughtfully, and he saw that something was on her mind.

"And when Daffy and Nevill have stopped quarrelling," added Eddy, "we'll have them established somewhere near by, and they shall come on the river too. We must fix that up somehow."

Molly said "Yes," again, and he asked, "And what's the matter now?" and touched a little pucker on her forehead with his finger. She smiled.

"I was only thinking, Eddy.... It was something Miss Hogan said, about spending Good Friday on the river. Do you think they really did?"

He laughed a little at her wide, questioning eyes and serious face.

"I suppose so. But Bridget said 'Never again'—didn't you hear?"

"Oh yes. But that was only because of the crowd.... Of course it may be all right—but I just wished she hadn't said it, rather. It sounded as if they didn't care much, somehow. I'm sure they do, but...."

"I'm sure they don't," Eddy said. "Bridget isn't what you would call a Churchwoman, you see. Nor are Jane, or Arnold, or Billy. They see things differently, that's all."

"But—they're not dissenters, are they?"

Eddy laughed. "No. That's the last thing any of them are."

Molly's wide gaze became startled.

"Do you mean—they're heathens? Oh, how dreadfully sad, Eddy. Can't you ... can't you help them somehow? Couldn't you ask some clergyman you know to meet them?"

Eddy chuckled again. "I'm glad I'm engaged to you, Molly. You please me. But I'm afraid the clergyman would be no more likely to convert them than they him."

Molly remembered something Daphne had once told her about Miss Dawn and Mrs. Le Moine and the prayer book. "It's so dreadfully sad," she repeated. There was a little silence. The revelation was working in Molly's mind. She turned it over and over.

"Eddy."

"Molly?"

"Don't you find it matters? In being friends, I mean?"

"What? Oh, that. No, not a bit. How should it matter, that I happen to believe certain things they don't? How could it?"

"It would to me." Molly spoke with conviction. "I might try, but I know I couldn't really be friends—not close friends—with an unbeliever."

"Oh yes, you could. You'd get over all that, once you knew them. It doesn't stick out of them, what they don't believe; it very seldom turns up. Besides theirs is such an ordinary, and such a comprehensible and natural point of view. Have you always believed what you do now about such things?"

"Why, of course. Haven't you?"

"Oh dear no. For quite a long time I didn't. After all, it's pretty difficult.... And particularly at my home I think it was a little difficult—for me, anyhow. I suppose I wanted more of the Catholic Church standpoint. I didn't come across that much till Cambridge; then suddenly I caught on to the point of view, and saw how fine it was."

"It's more than fine," said Molly. "It's true."

"Rather, of course it is. So are all fine things. If once all these people who don't believe saw the fineness of it, they'd see it must be true. Meanwhile, I don't see that the fact that one believes one's friends to be missing something they might have is any sort of reason for not being friends. Is it now? Billy might as well say he couldn't be friends with you because you said you didn't care about Masefield. You miss something he's got; that's all the difference it makes, in either case."

"Masefield isn't so important as——" Molly left a shy hiatus.

"No; of course; but, it's the same principle.... Well, anyhow you like them, don't you?" said Eddy shifting his ground.

"Oh, yes, I do. But I expect they think me a duffer. I don't know anything about their things, you see. They're awfully nice to me."

"That seems odd, certainly. And they may come and visit us at the Osiers, mayn't they?"

"Of course. And we'll all have tea on the balcony there. Oh, do let's begin turning out the people that live there at once."

Meanwhile Jane and Arnold and Billy, walking along the embankment, when they had discussed the colour of the water, the prospects of the weather, the number of cats on the wall, and other interesting subjects, commented on Molly. Jane said, "She's a little sweetmeat. I love her yellow eyes and her rough curly hair. She's like a spaniel puppy we've got at home."

Billy said, "She's quite nice to talk to, too. I like her laugh."

Arnold said, maliciously, "She'll never read your poetry, Billy. She probably only reads Tennyson's and Scott's and the *Anthology of Nineteenth Century Verse*."

"Well," said Billy, placidly, "I'm in that. If she knows that, she knows all the best twentieth century poets. You seem to be rather acrimonious about her. Hadn't she read your 'Latter Day Leavings,' or what?"

"I'm sure I trust not. She'd hate them.... It's all very well, and I've no doubt she's a very nice little girl—but what does Eddy want with marrying her? Or, indeed, anyone else? He's not old enough to settle down. And marrying that spaniel-child will mean settling down in a sense."

"Oh, I don't know. She's got plenty of fun, and can play all right."

Arnold shook his head over her. "All the same, she's on the side of darkness and the conventions. She mayn't know it yet, being still half a child, and in the playing puppy stage, but give her ten years and you'll see. She'll become proper. Even now, she's not sure we're quite nice or very good. I spotted that.... Don't you remember, Jane, what I said to you at Welchester about it? With my never-failing perspicacity, I foresaw the turn events would take, and I foresaw also exactly how she would affect Eddy. You will no doubt recollect what I said (I hope you always do); therefore I won't repeat it now, even for Billy's sake. But I may tell you, Billy, that I prophesied the worst. I still prophesy it."

"You're too frightfully particular to live, Arnold," Billy told him. "She's a very good sort and a very pleasant person. Rather like a brook in sunlight, I thought her; her eyes are that colour, and her hair and dress are the shadowed parts, and her laugh is like the water chuckling over a stone. I like her."

"Oh, heavens," Arnold groaned. "Of course you do. You and Jane are hopeless. You may *like* brooks in sunlight or puppies or anything else in the universe—but you don't want to go and *marry* them because of that."

"I don't," Billy admitted, peacefully. "But many people do. Eddy obviously is one of them. And I should say it's quite a good thing for him to do."

"Of course it is," said Jane, who was more interested at the moment in the effect of the evening mist on the river.

"Perhaps they'll think better of it and break it off before the wedding-day," Arnold gloomily suggested. "There's always that hope.... I see no place for this thing called love in a reasonable life. It will smash up Eddy, as it's smashed up Eileen. I hate the thing."

"Eileen's a little better lately," said Jane presently. "She's going to play at Lovinski's concert next week."

"She's rather worse really," said Billy, a singularly clear-sighted person; and they left it at that.

Billy was very likely right. At that moment Eileen was lying on the floor of her room, her head on her flung-out arms, tearless and still, muttering a name over and over, through clenched teeth. The passage of time took her further from him, slow hour by slow hour; took her out into cold, lonely seas of pain, to drown uncomforted. She was not rather better.

She would spend long mornings or evenings in the fields and lanes by the Lea, walking or sitting, silent and alone. She never went to the disorganised, lifeless remnant of Datcherd's settlement; only she would travel by the tram up Shoreditch and Mare Street to the north east, and walk along the narrow path by the Lea-side wharf cottages, little and old and jumbled, and so over the river on to Leyton Marsh, where sheep crop the grass. Here she and Datcherd had often walked, after an evening at the Club, and here she now wandered alone. These regions have a queer, perhaps morbid, peace; they brood, as it were, on the fringe of the huge world of London; they divide it, too, from that other stranger, sadder world beyond the Lea, Walthamstow and its endless drab slums.

Here, in the November twilight on Leyton Marsh, Eddy found her once. He himself was bicycling back from Walthamstow, where he had been to see one of his Club friends (he had made many) who lived there. Eileen was leaning on a stile at the end of one of the footpaths that thread this strange borderland. They met face to face; and she looked at him as if she did not see him, as if she was expecting someone not him. He got off his bicycle, and said "Eileen."

She looked at him dully, and said, "I'm waiting for Hugh."

He gently took her hand. "You're cold. Come home with me."

Her dazed eyes upon his face slowly took perception and meaning, and with them pain rushed in. She shuddered horribly, and caught away her hand.

"Oh ... I was waiting ... but it's no use ... I suppose I'm going mad...."

"No. You're only tired and unstrung. Come home now, won't you. Indeed you mustn't stay."

The mists were white and chilly about them; it was a strange phantom world, set between the million-eyed monster to the west, and the smaller, sprawling, infinitely sad monster to the east.

She flung out her arms to the red-eyed city, and moaned, "Hugh, Hugh, Hugh," till she choked and cried.

Eddy bit his own lips to steady them. "Eileen—dear Eileen—come home. He'd want you to."

She returned, through sobs that rent her. "He wants nothing any more. He always wanted things, and never got them; and now he's dead, the way he can't even want. But I want him; I want him; I want him—oh, Hugh!"

So seldom she cried, so strung up and tense had she long been, even to the verge of mental delusion, that now that a breaking-point had come, she broke utterly, and cried and cried, and could not stop.

He stood by her, saying nothing, waiting till he could be of use. At last from very weariness she quieted, and stood very still, her head bowed on her arms that were flung across the stile.

He said then, "Dear, you will come now, won't you," and apathetically she lifted her head, and her dim, wet, distorted face was strange in the mist-swathed moonlight.

Together they took the little path back over the grass-grown marsh, where phantom sheep coughed in the fog, and so across the foot-bridge to the London side of the Lea, and the little wharfside cottages, and up on to the Lea Bridge Road, and into Mare Street, and there, by unusual good fortune there strayed a taxi, a rare phenomenon north of Shoreditch, and Eddy put Eileen and himself and his bicycle in it and on it, and so they came back out of the wilds of the east, by Liverpool Street and the city, across London to Campden Hill Road in the further west. And all the way Eileen leant back exhausted and very still, only shuddering from time to time, as one does after a fit of crying or of sickness. But by the end of the journey she was a little restored. Listlessly she touched Eddy's hand with her cold one.

"Eddy, you are a dear. You've been good to me, and I such a great fool. I'm sorry. It isn't often I am.... But I think if you hadn't come to-night I would have gone mad, no less. I was on the way there, I believe. Thank you for saving me. And now you'll come in and have something, won't you."

He would not come in. He should before this have been at Mrs. Crawford's for dinner. He waited to see her in, then hurried back to Soho to dress. His last sight of her was as she turned to him in the doorway, the light on her pale, tear-marred face, trying to smile to cheer him. That was a good sign, he believed, that she could think even momentarily of anyone but herself and the other who filled her being.

Heavy-hearted for pity and regret, he drove back to his rooms and hurriedly dressed, and arrived in Hyde Park Terrace desperately late, a thing Mrs. Crawford found it hard to forgive. In fact, she did not try to forgive it. She said, "Oh, we had quite given up hope. Hardwick, some soup for Mr. Oliver."

Eddy said he would rather begin where they had got to. But he was not allowed thus to evade his position, and had to hurry through four courses before he caught them up. They were a small party, and he apologised across the table to his hostess as he ate.

"I'm frightfully sorry; simply abject. The fact is, I met a friend on Leyton Marsh."

"On *what*?"

"Leyton Marsh. Up in the north east, by the Lea, you know."

"I certainly don't know. Is that where you usually take your evening walks when dining in Kensington?"

"Well, sometimes. It's the way to Walthamstow, you see. I know some people there."

"Really. You do, as the rationalist bishop told you, touch a very extensive circle, certainly. And so you met one of them on this marsh, and the pleasure of their society was such——"

"She wasn't well, and I took her back to where she lived. She lives in Kensington, so it took ages; then I had to get back to Compton Street to dress. Really, I'm awfully sorry."

Mrs. Crawford's eyebrows conveyed attention to the sex of the friend; then she resumed conversation with the barrister on her right.

Molly said consolingly, "Don't you mind, Eddy. She doesn't really. She only pretends to, for fun. She knows it wasn't your fault. Of course you had to take your friend home if she wasn't well."

"I couldn't have left her, as a matter of fact. She was frightfully unhappy and unhinged.... It was Mrs. Le Moine." He conquered a vague reluctance and added this. He was not going to have the vestige of a secret from Molly.

She flushed quickly and said nothing, and he knew that he had hurt her. Yet it was an unthinkable alternative to conceal the truth from her; equally unthinkable not to do these things that hurt her. What then, would be the solution? Simply he did not know. A change of attitude on her part seemed to him the only possible one, and he had waited now long for that in vain. To avert her sombreness and his, he began to talk cheerfully to her about all manner of things, and she responded, but not quite spontaneously. A shadow lay between them.

So obvious was it that after dinner he told her so, in those words.

She tried to smile. "Does it? How silly you are."

"You'd better tell me the worst, you know. You think it was ill-bred of me to be late for dinner."

"What rubbish; I don't. As if you could help it."

But he knew she thought he could have helped it. So they left it at that, and the shadow remained.

Eddy, it may have been mentioned, had the gift of sympathy largely developed—the quality of his defect of impressionability. He had it more than is customary. People found that he said and felt the most consoling thing, and left unsaid the less. It was because he found realisation easy. So people in trouble often came to him. Eileen Le Moine, reaching out in her desperate need on the mist-bound marshes, had, as it were, met the saving grasp of his hand. Half-consciously she had let it draw her out of the deep waters where she was sinking, on to the shores of sanity. She reached out to him again. He had cared for Hugh; he cared for her; he understood how nothing in heaven and earth now mattered; he did not try to give her interests; he simply gave her his sorrow and understanding and his admiration of Hugh. So she claimed it, as a drowning man clutches instinctively at the thing which will best support him. And as she claimed he gave. He gave of his best. He tried to make Molly give too, but she would not.

There came a day when Bridget Hogan wrote and said that she had to go out of town for Sunday, and didn't want to leave Eileen alone in the flat all day, and would Eddy come and see her there—come to lunch, perhaps, and stay for the afternoon.

"You are good for her; better than anyone else, I think," Bridget wrote. "She feels she can talk about Hugh to you, though to hardly anyone—not even to me much. I am anxious about her just now. Please do come if you can."

Eddy, who had been going to lunch and spend the afternoon at the Crawfords', made no question about it. He went to Molly and told her how it was. She listened silently. The room was strange with fog and blurred lights, and her small grave face was strange and pale too.

Eddy said, "Molly, I wish you would come too, just this once. She would love it; she would indeed.... Just this once, Molly, because she's in such trouble. Will you?"

Molly shook her head, and he somehow knew it was because she did not trust her voice.

"Well, never mind, then, darling. I'll go alone."

Still she did not speak. After a moment he rose to go. He took her cold hands in his, and would have kissed her, but she pushed him back, still wordless. So for a moment they stood, silent and strange and perplexed in the blurred fog-bound room, hands locked in hands.

Then Molly spoke, steady-voiced at last.

"I want to say something, Eddy. I must, please."

"Do, sweetheart."

She looked at him, as if puzzled by herself and him and the world, frowning a little, childishly.

"We can't go on, Eddy. I ... I can't go on."

Cold stillness fell over him like a pall. The fog-shadows huddled up closer round them.

"What do you mean, Molly?"

"Just that. I can't do it.... We mustn't be engaged any more."

"Oh, yes, we must. I must, you must. Molly, don't talk such ghastly nonsense. I won't have it. Those aren't things to be said between you and me, even in fun."

"It's not in fun. We mustn't be engaged any more, because we don't fit. Because we make each other unhappy. Because, if we married, it would be worse. No—listen now; it's only this once and for all, and I must get it all out; don't make it more difficult than it need be, Eddy. It's because you have friends I can't ever have; you care for people I must always think bad; I shall never fit into your set.... The very fact of your caring for them and not minding what they've done, proves we're miles apart really."

"We're not miles apart." Eddy's hands on her shoulders drew her to him. "We're close together—like this. And all the rest of the world can go and drown itself. Haven't we each other, and isn't it enough?"

She pulled away, her two hands against his breast.

"No, it isn't enough. Not enough for either of us. Not for me, because I can't not mind that you think differently from me about things. And not for you, because you want—you need to have—all the rest of the world too. You don't mean that about its drowning itself. If you did, you wouldn't be going to spend Sunday with——"

"No, I suppose I shouldn't. You're right. The rest of the world mustn't drown itself, then; but it must stand well away from us and not get in our way."

"And you don't mean that, either," said Molly, strangely clear-eyed. "You're not made to care only for one person—you need lots. And if we were married, you'd either have them, or you'd be cramped and unhappy. And you'd want the people I can't understand or like. And you'd want me to like them, and I couldn't. And we should both be miserable."

"Oh, Molly, Molly, are we so silly as all that? Just trust life—just live it—don't let's brood over it and map out all its difficulties beforehand. Just trust it—and trust love—isn't love good enough for a pilot?—and we'll take the plunge together."

She still held him away with her pressing hands, and whispered, "No, love isn't good enough. Not—not your love for me, Eddy."

"*Not?*"

"No." Quite suddenly she weakened and collapsed, and her hands fell from him, and she hid her face in them and the tears came.

"No—don't touch me, or I can't say it. I know you care ... but there are so many ways of caring. There's the way you care for me ... and the way ... the way you've always cared for ... her...."

Eddy stood and looked down at her as she crouched huddled in a chair, and spoke gently.

"There *are* many ways of caring. Perhaps one cares for each of one's friends rather differently—I don't know. But love is different from them all. And I love you, Molly. I have loved no one else, ever, in that sense.... I'm not going to pretend I don't understand you. By 'her' I believe you mean Eileen Le Moine. Now can you look me in the face and say you think I care for Eileen Le Moine in—in that way? No, of course you can't. You know I don't; what's more, you know I never did. I have always admired her, liked her, been fond of her, attracted to her. If you asked why I have never fallen in love with her, I suppose I should answer that it was, in the first instance, because she never gave me the chance. She has always, since I knew her, been so manifestly given over, heart and soul, to someone else. To fall in love with her would have been absurd. Love needs just the element of potential reciprocity; at least, for me it does. There was never that element with Eileen. So I never—quite—fell in love with her. That perhaps was my reason before I found I cared for you. After that, no reason was needed. I had found the real thing.... And now you talk of taking it away from me. Molly, say you don't mean it; say so at once, please." She had stopped crying, and sat huddled in the big chair, with downbent, averted face.

"But I do mean it, Eddy." Her voice came small and uncertain through the fog-choked air. "Truly I do. You see, the things I hate and can't get over are just nothing at all to you. We don't feel the same about right and wrong.... There's religion, now. You want me, and you'd want me more if we were married, to be friends with people who haven't any, in the sense I mean, and don't want any. Well, I can't. I've often told you. I suppose I'm made that way. So there it is; it wouldn't be happy a bit, for either of us.... And then there are the wrong things people do, and which you don't mind. Perhaps I'm a prig, but anyhow we're different, and I do mind. I shall always mind. And I shouldn't like to feel I was getting in the way of your having the friends you liked, and we should have to go separate ways, and though you could be friends with all my friends—because you can with everyone—I couldn't with all yours, and we should hate it. You want so many more kinds of things and people than I do; I suppose that's it." (Arnold Denison, who had once said, "Her share of the world is homogeneous; his is heterogeneous," would perhaps have been surprised at her discernment, confirming his.)

Eddy said, "I want you. Whatever else I want, I want you. If you want me—if you did want me, as I thought you did—it would be enough. If you don't.... But you do, you must, you do."

And it was no argument. And she had reason and logic on her side, and he nothing but the unreasoning reason of love. And so through the dim afternoon they fought it out, and he came up against a will firmer than his own, holding both their loves in check, a vision clearer than his own, seeing life steadily and seeing it whole, till at last the vision was drowned in tears, and she sobbed to him to go, because she would talk no more. He went, vanquished and angry, out into the black, muffled city, and groped his way to Soho, like a man who has been robbed of his all and is full of bitterness but unbeaten, and means to get it back by artifice or force.

He went back next day, and the day after that, hammering desperately on the shut door of her resolve. The third day she left London and went home. He only saw Mrs. Crawford, who looked at him speculatively and with an odd touch of pity, and said, "So it's all over. Molly seems to know her own mind. I dislike broken engagements exceedingly; they are so noticeable, and give so much trouble. One would have thought that in all the years you have known each other one of you might have discovered your incompatibility before entering into rash compacts. But dear Molly only sees a little at a time, and that extremely clearly. She tells me you wouldn't suit each other. Well, she may be right, and anyhow I suppose she must be allowed to judge. But I am sorry."

She was kind; she hoped he would still come and see them; she talked, and her voice was far away and irrelevant. He left her. He was like a man who has been robbed of his all and knows he will never get it back, by any artifice or any force.

On Sunday he went to Eileen. It seemed about a month ago that he had heard from Bridget asking him to do so. He found her listless and heavy-eyed, and yawning from lack of sleep. Gently he led her to talk, till Hugh Datcherd seemed to stand alive in the room, caressed by their allusions. He told her of people who missed him; quoted what working-men of the Settlement had said of him; discussed his work. She woke from apathy. It was as if, among a world that, meaning kindness, bade her forget, this one voice bade her remember, and remembered with her; as if, among many voices that softened over his name as with pity for sadness and failure, this one voice rang glorying in his success. Sheer intuition had told Eddy that that was what she wanted, what she was sick for—some recognition, some triumph for him whose gifts had seemed to be broken and wasted, whose life had set in the greyness of unsuccess. As far as one man could give her what she wanted, he gave it, with both hands, and so she clung to him out of all the kind, uncomprehending world.

They talked far into the grey afternoon. And she grew better. She grew so much better that she said to him suddenly, "You look tired to death, do you know. What have you been doing to yourself?"

With the question and her concerned eyes, the need came to him in his turn for sympathy.

"I've been doing nothing. Molly has. She has broken off our engagement."

"Do you say so?" She was startled, sorry, pitiful. She forgot her own grief. "My dear—and I bothering you with my own things and never seeing how it was with you! How good you've been to me, Eddy. I wonder is there anyone else in the world would be so patient and so kind. Oh, but I'm sorry."

She asked no questions, and he did not tell her much. But to talk of it was good for both of them. She tried to give him back some of the sympathy she had had of him; she was only partly successful, being still half numbed and bound by her own sorrow; but the effort a little loosened the bands. And part of him watched their loosening with interest, as a doctor watches a patient's first motions of returning health, while the other part found relief in talking to her. It was a strange, half selfish, half unselfish afternoon they both had, and a little light crept in through the fogs that brooded about both of them. Eileen said as he went, "It's been dear of you to come like this.... I'm going to spend next Sunday at Holmbury St. Mary. If you're doing nothing else, I wish you'd come there too, and we'll spend the day tramping."

Her thought was to comfort both of them, and he accepted it gladly. The thought came to him that there was no one now to mind how he spent his Sundays. Molly would have minded. She would have thought it odd, not proper, hardly right. Having lost her partly on this very account, he threw himself with the more fervour into this mission of help and healing to another and himself. His loss did not thus seem such utter waste, the emptiness of the long days not so blank.

CHAPTER XIV.

UNITY.

THE office of *Unity* was a room on the top floor of the Denisons' publishing house. It looked out on Fleet Street, opposite Chancery Lane. Sitting there, Eddy, when not otherwise engaged (he and Arnold were joint editors of *Unity*) watched the rushing tide far below, the people crowding by. There with the tide went the business men, the lawyers, the newspaper people, who made thought and ensued it, the sellers and the buyers. Each had his and her own interests, his and her own irons in the fire. They wanted none of other people's; often they resented other people's. Yet, looked at long enough ahead (one of the editors in his trite way mused) all interests must be the same in the end. No state, surely, could thrive, divided into factions, one faction spoiling another. They must needs have a common aim, find a heterogeneous city of peace. So *Unity*, gaily flinging down barriers, cheerily bestriding walls, with one foot planted in each neighbouring and antagonistic garden—*Unity*, so sympathetic with all causes, so ably written, so versatile, must surely succeed.

Unity really was rather well written, rather interesting. New magazines so often are. The co-operative contributors, being clever people, and fresh-minded, usually found some new, unstaled aspect of the topics they touched, and gave them life. The paper, except for a few stories and poems and drawings, was frankly political and social in trend; it dealt with current questions, not in the least impartially (which is so dull), but taking alternate and very definite points of view. Some of these articles were by the staff, others by specialists. Not afraid to aim high, they endeavoured to get (in a few cases succeeded, in most failed) articles by prominent supporters and opponents of the views they handled; as, for example, Lord Hugh Cecil and Dr. Clifford on Church Disestablishment; Mr. Harold Cox and Sir William Robertson Nicholl on Referendums, Dr. Cunningham and Mr. Strachey on Tariff Reform; Mr. Roger Fry and Sir William Richmond on Art; Lord Robert Cecil and the Sidney Webbs on the Minimum Wage; the Dean of Welchester and Mr. Hakluyt Egerton on Prayer Book Revision; Mr. Conrad Noel and Mr. Victor Grayson on Socialism as Synonymous with Christianity, an Employer, a Factory Hand, and Miss Constance Smith, on the Inspection of Factories; Mrs. Fawcett and Miss Violet Markham on Women as Political Creatures; Mr. J. M. Robertson and Monsignor R. H. Benson on the Church as an Agent for Good; land-owners, farmers, labourers, and Mr. F. E. Greene, on Land Tenure. (The farmers' and labourers' articles were among the failures, and had to be editorially supplied.) A paper's reach must exceed its grasp, or what are enterprising editors for? But *Unity* did actually grasp some writers of note, and some of unlettered ardour, and supplied, to fill the gaps in these, contributors of a certain originality and vividness of outlook. On the whole it was a readable production, as productions go. There were several advertisements on the last page; most, of course, were of books published by the Denisons, but there were also a few books published by other people, and, one proud week, "Darn No More," "Why Drop Ink," and "Dry Clean Your Dog." "Dry Clean Your Dog" seemed to the editors particularly promising; dogs, though led, indeed, by some literary people about the book-shops of towns, suggest in the main a wider, more breezy, less bookish class of reader; the advertisement called up a pleasant picture of *Unity* being perused in the country, perhaps even as far away as Weybridge, lying on hall tables along with the *Field* and *Country Life*, while its readers obediently repaired to the kennels with a dry shampoo.... It was an encouraging picture. For, though any new journal can get taken in (for a time) by the bookier cliques of cities, who read and write so much that they do not need to be very careful, in either case, what it is, how few shall force a difficult entrance into our fastidious country homes.

The editors of *Unity* could not, indeed, persuade themselves that they had a large circulation in the country as yet. Arnold said from the first, "We never shall have. That is very certain."

Eddy said, "Why?" He hoped they would have. It was his hope that *Unity* would circulate all round the English-speaking world.

"Because we don't stand for anything," said Arnold, and Eddy returned, "We stand for everything. We stand for Truth. We are of Use."

"We stand for a lot of lies, too," Arnold pointed out, because he thought it was lies to say that Tariff Reform and Referendums and Democracies were good things, and that Everyone should Vote, and that Plays should be Censored, and the Prayer Book Revised, and lots of other things. Eddy, who knew that Arnold knew that he for his part thought these things true, did not trouble to say so again.

Arnold added, "Not, of course, that standing for lies is any check on circulation; quite the contrary; but it's dangerous to mix them up with the truth; you confuse people's minds. The fact that I do not approve of any existing form of government or constitution of society, and that you approve of all, makes us harmonious collaborators, but hardly gives us, as an editorial body, enough insight into the mind of the average potential reader, who as a rule prefers, quite definitely prefers, one party or one state of things to another; has, in fact, no patience with any other, and does not in the least wish to be told how admirable it is. And if he does—if a country squire, for instance, really does want to hear a eulogy of Free Trade—(there may be a few such squires, possibly, hidden in the home counties; I doubt it, but there may)—well, there is the *Spectator* ready to his hand. The *Spectator*, which has the incidental advantage of not disgusting him on the next page with 'A Word for a Free Drama,' or 'Socialism as Synonymous with Christianity.' If, on the other hand, as might conceivably happen, he desired to hear the praises of Tariff Reform—well, there are the *Times* and the *Morning Post*, both organs that he knows and trusts. And if, by any wild chance, in an undisciplined mood, he craved for an attack on the censorship, or other insubordinate sentiments, he might find at any rate a few to go on with in, say, the *English Review*. Or, if it is Socialism he wants to hear about (and I never yet met the land-owner, did you, who hadn't Socialism on the brain; it's a class obsession), there is the *New Statesman*, so bright, thorough, and reliable. Or, if he wants to learn the point of view and the grievances of his tenant farmers or his agricultural labourers, without asking them, he can read books on 'The Tyranny of the Countryside,' or take in the *Vineyard*. Anyhow, where does *Unity* come in? I don't see it, I'm afraid. It would be different if we were merely or mainly literary, but we're frankly political. To be political without being partisan is savourless, like an egg without salt. It doesn't go down. Liberals don't like, while reading a paper, to be hit in the eye by long articles headed 'Toryism as the only Basis.' Unionists don't care to open at a page inscribed 'The Need for Home Rule.' Socialists object to being confronted by articles on 'Liberty as an Ideal.' No one wants to see exploited and held up for admiration the ideals of others antagonistic to their own. You yourself wouldn't read an article—not a long article, anyhow—called 'Party Warfare as the Ideal.' At least you might, because you're that kind of lunatic, but few would. That is why we shall not sell well, when people have got over buying us because we're new."

Eddy merely said, "We're good. We're interesting. Look at this drawing of Jane's; and this thing of Le Moine's. They by themselves should sell us, as mere art and literature. There are lots of people who'll let us have any politics we like if we give them things as good as that with them."

But Arnold jeered at the idea of there being enough readers who cared for good work to make a paper pay. "The majority care for bad, unfortunately."

"Well, anyhow," said Eddy, "the factory articles are making a stir among employers. Here's a letter that came this morning."

Arnold read it.

"He thinks it's his factory we meant, apparently. Rather annoyed, he sounds. 'Does not know if we purpose a series on the same subject'—nor if so what's going to get put into it, I suppose. I imagine he suspects one of his own hands of being the author. It wasn't, though, was it; it was a jam man. And very temperate in tone it was; most unreasonable of any employer to cavil at it. The remarks were quite general, too; mainly to the effect that all factories were unwholesome, and all days too long; statements that can hardly be disputed even by the proudest employer. I expect he's more afraid of what's coming than of what's come already."

"Anyhow," said Eddy, "*he's* coming. In about ten minutes, too. Shall I see him, or you?"

"Oh, you can. What does he want out of us?"

"I suppose he wants to know who wrote the article, and if we purpose a series. I shall tell him we do, and that I hope the next number of it will be an article by him on the Grievances of Employers. We need one, and it ought to sweeten him. Anyhow it will show him we've no prejudice in the matter. He can say all workers are pampered and all days too short, if he likes. I should think that would be him coming up now."

It was not him, but a sturdy and sweet-faced young man with an article on the Irrelevance of the Churches to the World's Moral Needs. The editors, always positive, never negative, altered the title to the Case for Secularism. It was to be set next to an article by a Church Socialist on Christianity the Only Remedy. The sweet-faced young man objected to this, but was over-ruled. In the middle of the discussion came the factory owner, and Eddy was left alone to deal with him. After that as many of the contributors as found it convenient met at lunch at the Town's End Tavern, as they generally did on Fridays, to discuss the next week's work.

This was at the end of January, when *Unity* had been running for two months. The first two months of a weekly paper may be significant, but are not conclusive. The third month is more so. Mr. Wilfred Denison, who published *Unity*, found the third month conclusive enough for him. He said so. At the Town's End on a foggy Friday towards the end of February, Arnold and Eddy announced at lunch that *Unity* was going to stop. No one was surprised. Most of these people were journalists, and used to these catastrophic births and deaths, so radiant or so sad, and often so abrupt. It is better when they are abrupt. Some die a long and lingering death, with many recuperations, artificial galvanisations, desperate recoveries, and relapses. The end is the same in either case; better that it should come quickly. It was an expected moment in this case, even to the day, for the contract with the contributors had been that the paper should run on its preliminary trial trip for three months, and then consider its position.

Arnold, speaking for the publishers, announced the result of the consideration.

"It's no good. We've got to stop. We're not increasing. In fact, we're dwindling. Now that people's first interest in a new thing is over, they don't buy us enough to pay our way."

"The advertisements are waning, certainly," said someone. "They're nearly all books and author's agencies and fountain pens now. That's a bad sign."

Arnold agreed. "We're mainly bought now by intellectuals and non-political people. As a political paper, we can't grow fat on that; there aren't enough of them.... We've discussed whether we should change our aim and become purely literary; but after all, that's not what we're out for, and there are too many of such papers already. We're essentially political and practical, and if we're to succeed as that, we've got to be partisan too, there's no doubt about it. Numbers of people have told us they don't understand our line, and want to know precisely what we're driving at politically. We reply we're driving at a union of parties, a throwing down of barriers. No one cares for that; they think it silly, and so do I. So, probably, do most of us: perhaps all of us except Oliver. Ned Jackson, for instance, was objecting the other day to my anti-Union article on the Docks strike appearing side by side with his own remarks of an opposite tendency. He, very naturally, would like *Unity* not merely to sing the praise of the Unions, but to give no space to the other side. I quite understand it; I felt the same myself. I extremely disliked his article; but the principles of the paper compelled us to take it. Why, my own father dislikes his essays on the Monistic Basis to be balanced by Professor Wedgewood's on Dualism as a Necessity of Thought. A philosophy, according to him, is either good or bad, true or false. So, to most people, are all systems of thought and principles of conduct. Very naturally, therefore, they prefer that the papers they read should eschew evil as well as seeking good. And so, since one can't (fortunately) read everything, they read those which seem to them to do so. I should myself, if I could find one which seemed to me to do so, only I never have.... Well, I imagine that's the sort of reason *Unity*'s failing; it's too comprehensive."

"It's too uneven on the literary and artistic side," suggested a contributor. "You can't expect working-men, for instance, who may be interested in the more practical side of the paper, to read it if it's liable to be weighted by Raymond's verse, or Le Moine's essays, or Miss Dawn's drawings. On the other hand, the clever people are occasionally shocked by coming on verse and prose suitable for working men. I expect it's that; you can't rely on it; it's not all of a piece, even on its literary side, like *Tit-Bits*, for instance. People like to know what to expect."

Cecil Le Moine said wearily in his high sweet voice, "Considering how few things do pay, I can't imagine why any of you ever imagined *Unity* would pay. I said from the first ... but no one listened to me; they never do. It's not *Unity*'s fault; it's the fault of all the other papers. There are hundreds too many already; millions too many. They want thinning, like dandelions in a garden, and instead, like dandelions, they spread like a disease. Something ought to be done about it. I hate Acts of Parliament, but this is really a case for one. It is surely Mr. McKenna's business to see to it; but I suppose he is kept too busy with all these vulgar disturbances. Anyhow, *we* have done our best now to stem the tide. There will be one paper less. Perhaps some of the others will follow our example. Perhaps the *Record* will. I met a woman in the train yesterday (between Hammersmith and Turnham Green it was), and I passed her my copy of *Unity* to read. I thought she would like to read my Dramatic Criticism, so it was folded back at that, but she turned over the pages till she came to something about the Roman Catholic Church, by some Monsignor; then she handed it back to me and said she always took the *Record*. She obviously supposed *Unity* to be a Popish organ. I hunted through it for some Dissenting sentiments, and found an article by a Welsh Calvinistic Methodist on Disestablishment, but it was too late;

she had got out. But there it is, you see; she always took the *Record*. They all always take something. There are too many.... Well, anyhow, can't we all ask each other to dinner one night, to wind ourselves up? A sort of funeral feast. Or ought the editors to ask the rest of us? Perhaps I shouldn't have spoken."

"You should not," Eddy said. "We were going to introduce that subject later on."

The company, having arranged the date of the dinner, and of the final business meeting, dispersed and got back to their several jobs. No one minded particularly about *Unity's* death, except Eddy. They were so used to that sort of thing, in the world of shifting fortunes in which writers for papers move.

But Eddy minded a good deal. For several months he had lived in and for this paper; he had loved it extraordinarily. He had loved it for itself, and for what, to him, it stood for. It had been his contribution to the cause that seemed to him increasingly of enormous importance; increasingly, as the failure of the world at large to appreciate it flung him from failure to failure, wrested opportunities one by one out of his grasp. People wouldn't realise that they were all one; that, surely, was the root difficulty of this distressed world. They would think that one set of beliefs excluded another; they were blind, they were rigid, they were mad. So they wouldn't read *Unity*, surely a good paper; so *Unity* must perish for lack of being wanted, poor lonely waif. Eddy rebelled against the sinking of the little ship he had launched and loved; it might, it would, had it been given a chance, have done good work. But its chance was over; he must find some other way.

To cheer himself up when he left the office at six o'clock, he went eastward, to see some friends he had in Stepney. But it did not cheer him up, for they were miserable, and he could not comfort them. He found a wife alone, waiting for her husband and sons, who were still out at the docks where they worked, though they ought to have been back an hour since. And they were blacklegs, and had refused to come out with the strikers. The wife was white, and red-eyed.

"They watch for them," she whimpered. "They lay and wait for them, and set on them, many to one, and do for them. There was someone 'eard a Union man say he meant to do for my men one day. I begged my man to come out, or anyhow to let the boys, but he wouldn't, and he says the Union men may go to 'ell for 'im. I know what'll be the end. There was a man drowned yesterday; they found 'im in the canal, 'is 'ands tied up; 'e wouldn't come out, and so they did for 'im, the devils. And it's just seven, and they stop at six."

"They've very likely stopped at the public for a bit on the way home," Eddy suggested gently, but she shook her head.

"They've not bin stoppin' anywhere since the strike began. Them as won't come out get no peace at the public.... The Union's a cruel thing, that it is, and my man and lads that never do no 'urt to nobody, they'll lay and wait for 'em till they can do for 'em.... There's Mrs. Japhet, in Jubilee Street; she's lost her young man; they knocked 'im down and kicked 'im to death on 'is way 'ome the other day. Of course 'e was a Jew, too, which made 'im more rightly disliked as it were; but it were because 'e wouldn't come out they did it. And there was Mrs. Jim Turner; they laid for 'er and bashed 'er 'ead in at the corner of Salmon Lane, to spite Turner. And they're so sly, the police can't lay 'ands on them, scarcely ever.... And it's gone seven, and as dark as 'ats."

She opened the door and stood listening and crying. At the end of the squalid street the trams jangled by along Commercial Road, bringing men and women home from work.

"They'll be all right if they come by tram," said Eddy.

"There's all up Jamaica Street to walk after they get out," she wailed.

Eddy went down the street and met them at the corner, a small man and two big boys, slouching along the dark street, Fred Webb and his sons, Sid and Perce. He had known them well last year at Datcherd's club; they were uncompromising individualists, and liberty was their watchword. They loathed the Union like poison.

Fred Webb said that there had been a bit of a row down at the docks, which had kept them. "There was Ben Tillett speaking, stirring them up all. They began hustling about a bit—but we got clear. The missus wants me to come out, but I'm not having any."

"Come out with that lot!" Sid added, in a rather unsteady voice. "I'd see them all damned first. *You* wouldn't say we ought to come out, Mr. Oliver, would you?"

Eddy said, "Well, not just now, of course. In a general way, I suppose there's some sense in it."

"Sense!" growled Webb. "Don't you go talking to my boys like that, sir, if you please. You're not going to come out, Sid, so you needn't think about it. Good night, Mr. Oliver."

Eddy, dismissed, went to see another Docks family he knew, and heard how the strike was being indefinitely dragged out and its success jeopardised by the blacklegs, who thought only for themselves.

"I hate a man not to have public spirit. The mean skunks. They'd let all the rest go to the devil just to get their own few shillings regular through the bad times."

"They've a right to judge for themselves, I suppose," said Eddy, and added a question as to the powers of the decent men to prevent intimidation and violence.

The man looked at him askance.

"Ain't no 'timidation or violence, as I know of. 'Course they say so; they'll say anything. Whenever a man gets damaged in a private quarrel they blame it on the Union chaps now. It's their opportunity. Pack o' liars, they are. 'Course a man may get hurt in a row sometimes; you can't help rows; but that's six of one and 'alf a dozen of the other, and it's usually the blacklegs as begin it. We only picket them, quite peaceful.... Judge for themselves, did you say? No, dang them; that's just what no man's a right to do. It's selfish; that's what it is.... I've no patience with these 'ere individualists."

Discovering that Eddy had, he shut up sullenly and suspiciously, and ceased to regard him as a friend, so Eddy left him. On the whole, it had not been a cheery evening.

He told Arnold about it when he got home.

"There's such a frightful lot to be said on both sides," he added.

Arnold said, "There certainly is. A frightful lot. If one goes down to the Docks any day one may hear a good deal of it being said; only that's nearly all on one side, and the wrong side.... I loathe the Unions and their whole system; it's revolting, the whole theory of the thing, quite apart from the bullying and coercion."

"I should rather like," said Eddy, "to go down to the Docks to-morrow and hear the men speaking. Will you come?"

"Well, I can't answer for myself; I may murder someone; but I'll come if you'll take the risk of that."

Eddy hadn't known before that Arnold, the cynical and negligent, felt so strongly about anything. He was rather interested.

"You've got to *have* Unions, surely you'd admit that," he argued. This began a discussion too familiar in outline to be retailed; the reasons for Unions and against them are both exceedingly obvious, and may be imagined as given. It lasted them till late at night.

They went down to the Docks next day, about six o'clock in the evening.

CHAPTER XV.

ARNOLD.

THERE was a crowd outside the Docks gates. Some, under the eyes of vigilant policemen, were picketing the groups of workmen as they came sullenly, nervously, defiantly, or indifferently out from the Docks. Others were listening to a young man speaking from a cart. Arnold and Eddy stopped to listen, too. It was poor stuff; not at all interesting. But it was adapted to its object and its audience, and punctuated by vehement applause. At the cheering, Arnold looked disgustedly on the ground; no doubt he was ashamed of the human race. But Eddy thought, "The man's a fool, but he's got hold of something sound. The man's a stupid man, but he's got brains on his side, and strength, and organisation; all the forces that make for civilisation. They're crude, they're brutal, they're revolting, these people, but they do look ahead, and that's civilisation." The Tory-Socialist side of him thus appreciated, while the Liberal-Individualist side applauded the blacklegs coming up from work. The human side applauded them, too; they were few among many, plucky men surrounded by murderous bullies, who would as likely as not track some of them home and bash their heads in on their own doorsteps, and perhaps their wives' heads too.

Eddy caught sight of Fred Webb and his two sons walking in a group, surrounded by picketters. Suddenly the scene became a nightmare to him, impossibly dreadful. Somehow he knew that people were going to hurt and be hurt very soon. He looked at the few police, and wondered at the helplessness or indifference of the law, that lets such things be, that is powerless to guard citizens from assault and murder.

He heard Arnold give a short laugh at his side, and recalled his attention to what the man on the cart was saying.

"The poor lunatic can't even make sense and logic out of his own case," Arnold remarked. "I could do it better myself."

Eddy listened. It was indeed pathetically stupid, pointless, sentimental.

After another minute of it, Arnold said, "Since they're so ready to listen, why shouldn't they listen to me for a change?" and scrambled up on to a cart full of barrels and stood for a moment looking round. The speaker went on speaking, but someone cried, "Here's another chap with something to say. Let 'im say it, mate; go on, young feller."

Arnold did go on. He had certainly got something to say, and he said it. For a minute or two the caustic quality of his utterances was missed; then it was slowly apprehended. Someone groaned, and someone else shouted, "Chuck it. Pull him down."

Arnold had a knack of biting and disagreeable speech, and he was using it. He was commenting on the weak points in the other man's speech. But if he had thought to persuade any, he was disillusioned. Like an audience of old, they cried out with a loud voice, metaphorically stopped their ears, and ran at him with one accord. Someone threw a brick at him. The next moment hands dragged him down and hustled him away. A voice Eddy recognised as Webb's cried, "Fair play; let 'im speak, can't you. 'E was talking sense, which is more than most here do."

The scuffling and hustling became excited and violent. It was becoming a free fight. Blacklegs were surrounded threateningly by strikers; the police drew nearer. Eddy pushed through shoving, angry men to get to Arnold. They recognised him as Arnold's companion, and hustled him about. Arnold was using his fists. Eddy saw him hit a man on the mouth. Someone kicked Eddy on the shin. He shot out his fist mechanically, and hit the man in the face, and thought, "I must have hurt him a lot, what a lot of right he's got on his side," before the blow was returned, cutting his lip open.

He saw Arnold disappear, borne down by an angry group; he pushed towards him, jostling through the men in his way, who were confusedly giving now before the mounted police. He could not reach Arnold; he lost sight of where he was; he was carried back by the swaying crowd. He heard a whimpering boy's voice behind him, "Mr. Oliver, sir," and looked round into young Sid Webb's sick, frightened face.

"They've downed dad.... And I think they've done for him.... They kicked him on the head.... They're after me now———"

Eddy said, "Stick near me," and the next moment Sid gave an angry squeal, because someone was twisting his arm back. Eddy turned round and hit a man under the chin, sending him staggering back under the feet of a plunging horse. The sight of the trampling hoofs so near the man's head turned Eddy sick; he swore and caught at the rein, and dragged the horse sharply sideways. The policeman riding it brought down his truncheon violently on his arm, which dropped nerveless and heavy at his side. Hands caught at his knees from below; he was dragged suddenly to the ground, and saw, looking up, the bleeding face of the man he had knocked down close to his own. The next moment the man was up, trampling him, pushing out of the way of the plunging horse. Eddy struggled to his knees, tried to get up, and could not. He was beaten down by a writhing forest of legs and heavy boots. He gave it up, and fell over on his side into the slimy, trodden mud. Everything hurt desperately—other people's feet, his own arm, his face, his body. The forest smelt of mud and human clothes, and suddenly became quite dark.

Someone was lifting his head, and trying to make him drink brandy. He opened his eyes and said, moving his cut lips stiffly and painfully, "Their principles are right, but their methods are rotten." Someone else said, "He's coming round," and he came.

He could breathe and see now, for the forest had gone. There were people still, and gas-lamps, and stars, but all remote. There were policemen, and he remembered how they had hurt him. It seemed, indeed, that everyone had hurt him. All their principles were no doubt right; but all their methods were certainly rotten.

"I'm going to get up," he said, and lay still.

"Where do you live?" asked someone. "Perhaps he'd better be taken to hospital."

Eddy said, "Oh, no. I live somewhere all right. Besides, I'm not hurt," but he could not talk well, because his mouth was so swollen. In another moment he remembered where he did live. "22A, Old Compton Street, of course." That reminded him of Arnold. Things were coming back to him.

"Where's my friend?" he mumbled. "He was knocked down, too."

They said, "Don't you worry about him; he'll be looked after all right," and Eddy sat up and said, "I suppose you mean he's dead," quietly, and with conviction.

Since that was what they did mean, they hushed him and told him not to worry, and he lay back in the mud and was quiet.

CHAPTER XVI.

EILEEN.

EDDY lay for some days in bed, battered and bruised, and slightly broken. He was not seriously damaged; not irreparably like Arnold; Arnold, who was beyond piecing together.

Through the queer, dim, sad days and nights, Eddy's weakened thoughts were of Arnold; Arnold the cynical, the sceptical, the supercilious, the scornful; Arnold, who had believed in nothing, and had yet been murdered for believing in something, and saying so. Arnold had hated democratic tyranny, and his hatred had given his words and his blows a force that had recoiled on himself and killed him. Eddy's blows on that chaotic, surprising evening had lacked this energy; his own consciousness of hating nothing had unnerved him; so he hadn't died. He had merely been buffeted about and knocked out of the way like so much rubbish by both combatant sides in turn. He bore the scars of the strikers' fists and boots, and of the heavy truncheon of the law. Both sides had struck him as an enemy, because he was not whole-heartedly for them. It was, surely, an ironical epitome, a brief summing-up in terms of blows, of the story of his life. What chaos, what confusion, what unheroic shipwreck of plans and work and career dogged those who fought under many colours! One died for believing in something; one didn't die for believing in everything; one lived on incoherently, from hand to mouth, despised of all, accepted of none, fruitful of nothing. For these the world has no use; the piteous, travailing world that needs all the helpers, all the workers it can get. The dim shadows of his room through the long, strange nights seemed to be walls pressing round, pressing in closer and closer, pushed by the insistent weight of the unredressed evil without. Here he saw himself lying, shut by the shadow walls into a little secluded place, allowed to do nothing, because he was no use. The evil without haunted his nightmares; it must have bitten more deeply into his active waking moments than he had known. It seemed hideous to lie and do nothing. And when he wanted to get up at once and go out and do something to help, they would not let him. He was no use. He never would be any use.

More and more it seemed to him clear that the one way to be of use in this odd world—of the oddity of the world he was becoming increasingly convinced, comparing it with the many worlds he could more easily have imagined—the one way, it seemed, to be of use was to take a definite line and stick to it and reject all others; to be single-minded and ardent, and exclusive; to be, in brief, a partisan, if necessary a bigot. In procession there moved before him the fine, strong, ardent people he had known, who had spent themselves for an idea, and for its inherent negations, and he saw them all as martyrs; Eileen, living on broken and dead because so utter had been her caring for one person that no one else was any good; Molly, cutting two lives apart for a difference of principle; Billy Raymond, Jane Dawn, all the company of craftsmen and artists, fining words and lines to their utmost, fastidiously rejecting, laying down insuperable barriers between good and bad, so that never the twain should meet; priests and all moral reformers, working against odds for these same barriers in a different sphere; all workers, all artists, all healers of evil, all makers of good; even Daphne and Nevill, parted for principles that could not join; and Arnold, dead for a cause. Only the aimless drifters, the ineptitudes, content to slope through the world on thoughts, were left outside the workshop unused.

In these dark hours of self-disgust, Eddy half thought of becoming a novelist, that last resource of the spiritually destitute. For novels are not life, that immeasurably important thing that has to be so sternly approached; in novels one may take as many points of view as one likes, all at the same time; instead of working for life, one may sit and survey it from all angles simultaneously. It is only when one starts walking on a road that one finds it excludes the other roads. Yes; probably he would end a novelist. An ignoble, perhaps even a fatuous career; but it is, after all, one way through this queer, shifting chaos of unanswerable riddles. When solutions are proved unattainable, some spend themselves and their all on a rough-and-ready shot at truth, on doing what they can with the little they know; others give it up and talk about it. It was as a refuge for such as these that the novelist's trade was presented to man, we will not speculate from whence or by whom....

Breaking into these dark reflections came friends to see him, dropping in one by one. The first was Professor Denison, the morning after the accident. A telegram had brought him up from Cambridge, late last night. Seeing his grey, stricken face, Eddy felt miserably disloyal, to have come out of it alive. Dr. Denison patted him on the shoulder and said, "Poor boy, poor boy. It is hard for you," and it was Eddy who had tears in his eyes.

"I took him there," he muttered; but Dr. Denison took no notice of that.

Eddy said next, "He spoke so splendidly," then remembered that Arnold had spoken on the wrong side, and that that, too, must be bitter to his father.

Professor Denison made a queer, hopeless, deprecatory gesture with his hands.

"He was murdered by a cruel system," he said, in his remote, toneless voice. "Don't think I blame those ignorant men who did him to death. What killed him was the system that made those men what they are—the cruel oppression, the economic grinding—what can you expect...." He broke off, and turned helplessly away, remembering only that he had lost his son.

Every day as long as he stayed in London he came into Eddy's room after visiting Arnold's, and sat with him, infinitely gentle, silent, and sad.

Mrs. Oliver said, "Poor man, one's too dreadfully sorry for him to suggest it, but it's not the best thing for you to have him, dear."

The other visitors who came were probably better for Eddy, but Mrs. Oliver thought he had too many. All his friends seemed to come all day.

And once Eileen Le Moine came, and that was not as it should be. Mrs. Oliver, when the message was sent up, turned to Eddy doubtfully; but he said at once, "Ask her if she'll come up," and she had to bear it.

Mrs. Le Moine came in. Mrs. Oliver slightly touched her hand. For a moment her look hung startled on the changed, dimmed brilliance she scarcely recognised. Mrs. Le Moine, whatever her sins, had, it seemed, been through desperate times since they had parted at Welchester fourteen months ago. There was an absent look about her, as if she scarcely took in Eddy's mother. But for Eddy himself, stretched shattered on the couch by the fire, her look was pitiful and soft.

Mrs. Oliver's eyes wavered from her to Eddy. Being a lady of kind habits, she usually left Eddy alone with his friends for a little. In this instance she was doubtful; but Eddy's eyes, unconsciously wistful, decided her, and she yielded. After all, a three-cornered interview between them would have been a painful absurdity. If Eddy must have such friends, he must have them to himself....

When they were alone, Eileen sat down by him, still a little absent and thoughtful, though, bending compassionate eyes on him, she said softly, of him and Arnold, "You poor boys...." Then she was broodingly silent, and seemed to be casting about how to begin.

Suddenly she pulled herself together.

"We've not much time, have we? I must be quick. I've something I want to say to you, Eddy.... Do you know Mrs. Crawford came to see me the other day?"

Eddy shook his head, languidly, moved only with a faint surprise at Mrs. Crawford's unexpectedness.

Eileen went on, "I just wondered had she told you. But I thought perhaps not.... I like her, Eddy. She was nice to me. I don't know why, because I supposed—but never mind. What she came for was to tell me some things. Things I think I ought to have guessed for myself. I think I've been very stupid and very selfish, and I complaining to you about my troubles all this long while, and never thinking how it might be doing you harm. I ought to have known why Molly broke your engagement."

"There were a number of reasons," said Eddy. "She thought we didn't agree about things and couldn't pull together."

Eileen shook her head. "She may have. But I think there was only one reason that mattered very much. She didn't approve of me, and didn't like it that you were my friend. And she was surely right. A man shouldn't have friends his wife can't be friends with too; it spoils it all. And of course she knew she couldn't be friends with me; she thinks me bad. Molly would find it impossible even if it wasn't wrong, to be friends with a bad person. So of course she had the engagement ended; there was no other way.... And you never told me it was that.... You should have told me, you foolish boy. Instead, you went on seeing me and being good to me, and letting me talk about my own things, and—and being just the one comfort I had, (for you have been that; it's the way you understand things, I suppose)—and I all the time spoiling your life. When Mrs. Crawford told me how it was I was angry with you. You had a right to have told me. And now I've come to tell *you* something. You're to go to Molly and mend what's broken, and tell her you and I aren't going to be friends any more. That will be the plain truth. We are not. Not friends to matter, I mean. We won't be seeing each other alone and meeting the way we've been doing. If we meet it will be by chance, and with other people; that won't hurt."

Eddy, red-faced and indignant, said weakly, "It will hurt. It will hurt me. Haven't I lost enough friends, then, that I must lose you, too?"

A queer little smile touched her lips.

"You have not. Not enough friends yet. Eddy, what's the best thing of all in this world of good things? Don't you and I both know it? Isn't it love, no less? And isn't love good enough to pay a price for? And if the price must be paid in coin you value—in friendship, and in some other good things—still, isn't it worth it? Ah, you know, and I know, that it is!"

The firelight, flickering across her white face, lit it swiftly to passion. She, who had paid so heavy a price herself, was saying what she knew.

"So you'll pay it, Eddy. You'll pay it. You'll have to pay more than you know, before you've done with love. I wonder will you have to pay your very soul away? Many people have to do that; pay away their own inmost selves, the things in them they care for most, their secret dreams. 'I have laid my dreams under your feet. Tread softly, because you tread on my dreams.'... It's like that so often; and then she—or he—doesn't always tread softly; they may tread heavily, the way the dreams break and die. Still, it's worth it...."

She fell into silence, brooding with bent head and locked hands. Then she roused herself, and said cheerfully, "You may say just what you like, Eddy, but I'm not going to spoil your life any more. That's gone on too long already. If it was only by way of saying thank you, I would stop it now. For you've been a lot of use to me, you know. I don't think I could easily tell you how much. I'm not going to try; only I *am* going to do what I can to help you patch up your affairs that you've muddled so. So you go to Molly directly you get home, and make her marry you. And you'll pay the price she asks, and you'll go on, both of you, paying it and paying it, more and more of it, as long as you both live."

"She won't have me," said Eddy. "No one would have me, I should think. Why should they? I'm nothing. Everyone else is something; but I'm nothing. I can do nothing, and be nothing. I am a mere muddle. Why should Molly, who is straight and simple and direct, marry a muddle?"

"Because," said Eileen, "she cares for it. And she'll probably straighten it out a bit; that's what I mean, partly, by the price ... you'll have to become straight and simple and direct too, I wouldn't wonder, in the end. You may die a Tory country gentleman, no less, saying, 'To hell with these Socialist thieves'—no, that's the horrid language we use in Ireland alone isn't it, but I wouldn't wonder if the English squires meant the same. Or you might become equally simple and direct in another direction, and say, 'Down with the landed tyrants,' only Molly wouldn't like that so well. But it'll be a wonder if you don't, once you're married to Molly, have to throw overboard a few creeds, as well as a few people. Anyhow, that's not your business now. What you've got to do now is to get your health again and go down to Welchester and talk to Molly the way she'll see reason.... And now I must go. Your mother doesn't care for me to be here, but I had to come this once; it's never again, you can tell her that."

Eddy sat up and frowned. "Don't go on like that, Eileen. I've not the least intention of having my friendships broken for me like this. If Molly ever marries me—only she won't—it will be to take my friends; that is certain."

She shook her head and smiled down on him as she rose.

"You'll have to let your friends settle whether they want to be taken or not, Eddy.... Dear, kind, absurd boy, that's been so good to me, I'm going now. Goodbye, and get well."

Her fingers lightly touched his forehead, and she left him; left him alone in a world become poor and thin and ordinary, shorn of some beauty, of certain dreams and laughter and surprises.

Into it came his mother.

"Is Mrs. Le Moine gone, then, dear?"

"Yes," he said. "She is gone."

So flatly he spoke, so apathetically, that she looked at him in anxiety.

"She has tired you. You have been talking too much. Really, this mustn't happen again...."

He moved restlessly over on to his side.

"It won't happen again, mother. Never again."

CHAPTER XVII.

CONVERSION.

ON Midsummer Eve, which was the day before his marriage, Eddy had a number of his friends to dinner at the Moulin d'Or. It had amused him to ask a great many, and to select them from many different quarters and sets, and to watch how they all got on together. For many of them were not in the habit of meeting one another. The Vicar of St. Gregory's, for instance, did not, in the normal course of his days, as a rule come across Billy Raymond, or Cecil Le Moine, with whom he was conversing courteously across the table; Bob Traherne, his curate, seldom chatted affably with Conservative young members of Parliament such as Nevill Bellairs; Mrs. Crawford had long since irrevocably decided against social intercourse with Eileen Le Moine, to whom she was talking this evening as if she was rather pleased to have the opportunity; Bridget Hogan was wont to avoid militant desirers of votes, but to-night she was garrulously holding forth to a lady novelist of these habits who resided in a garden city; Eddy's friend, the young Irish Unionist, was confronted and probably outraged by Blake Connolly, Eileen's father, the Nationalist editor of the *Hibernian*, a vehement-tongued, hot-tempered, rather witty person, with deep blue eyes like Eileen's, and a flexible, persuasive voice. At the same table with Bob Traherne and Jane Dawn was a beautiful young man in a soft frilly shirt, an evangelical young man who at Cambridge had belonged to the C.I.C.C.U., and had preached in the Market Place. If he had known enough about them, he would have thought Jane Dawn's attitude towards religion and life a pity, and Bob Traherne's a bad mistake. But on this harmonious occasion they all met as friends. Even James Peters, sturdy and truthful, forbore to show Cecil Le Moine that he did not like him. Even Hillier, though it was pain and grief to him, kept silence from good words, and did not denounce Eileen Le Moine.

And Eddy, looking round the room at all of them, thought how well they all got on for one evening, because they were wanting to, and because one evening did not matter, and how they would not, many of them, get on at all, and would not even want to, if they were put to a longer test. And once again, at this, that he told himself was not the last, gathering of the heterogeneous crowd of his friends together, he saw how right they all were, in their different ways and yet at odds. He remembered how someone had said, "The interesting quarrels of the world are never between truth and falsehood, but between different truths." Ah, but must there be quarrels? More and more clearly he had come to see lately that there must; that through the fighting of extremes something is beaten out....

Someone thumped the table for silence, and Billy Raymond was on his feet, proposing their host's health and happiness. Billy was rather a charming speaker, in his unselfconscious, unfluent, amused, quietly allusive way, that was rather talk than speechifying. After him came Nevill Bellairs, Eddy's brother-in-law to be, who said the right things in his pleasant, cordial, well-bred, young member's manner. Then they drank Eddy's health, and after that Eddy got on to his feet to return thanks. But all he said was "Thanks very much. It was very nice of all of you to come. I hope you've all enjoyed this evening as much as I have, and I hope we shall have many more like it in future, after...." When he paused someone broke in with "He's a jolly good fellow," and they shouted it till the passers by in the Soho streets took it up and sang and whistled in chorus. That was the answer they unanimously gave to the hope he had expressed. It was an answer so cheerful and so friendly that it covered the fact that no one had echoed the hope, or even admitted it as a possibility. After all, it was an absurd thing to hope, for one dinner-party never is exactly like another; how should it be, with so much of life and death between?

When the singing and the cheering and the toasting was over, they all sat on and talked and smoked till late. Eddy talked too. And under his talking his perceptions were keenly working. The vivid, alive personalities of all these people, these widely differing men and women, boys and girls, struck sharply on his consciousness. There were vast differences between them, yet in nearly all was a certain fine, vigorous effectiveness, a power of achieving, getting something done. They all had their weapons, and used them in the battles of the world. They all, artists and philosophers, journalists and politicians, poets and priests, workers among the poor, players among the rich, knew what they would be at, where they thought they were going and how, and what they were up against. They made their choices; they selected, preferred, rejected ... hated.... The sharp, hard word brought him up. That was it; they hated. They all, probably, hated something or other. Even the tolerant, large-minded Billy, even the gentle Jane, hated what they considered bad literature, bad art. They not only sought good, but eschewed evil; if they had not realised the bad, the word "good" would have been meaningless to them.

With everyone in the room it was the same. Blake Connolly hated the Union—that was why he could be the force for Nationalism that he was; John Macleod, the Ulsterman, hated Nationalists and Papists—that was why he spoke so well on platforms for the Union; Bob Traherne hated capitalism—that was why he could fight so effectively for the economic betterment that he believed in; Nevill Bellairs hated Liberalism—that was why he got in at elections; the vicar of St. Gregory's hated disregard of moral laws—that was why he was a potent force for their observance among his parishioners; Hillier hated agnosticism—that was why he could tell his people without flinching that they would go to hell if they didn't belong to the Church; (he also, Eddy remembered, hated some writers of plays—and that, no doubt, was why he looked at Cecil Le Moine as he did;) Cecil Le Moine hated the commonplace and the stupid—that was why he never lapsed into either in his plays; Mrs. Crawford hated errors of breeding (such as discordant clothes, elopements, incendiarism, and other vulgar violence)—that was why her house was so select; Bridget Hogan hated being bored—that was why she succeeded in finding life consistently amusing; James Peters hated men of his own class without collars, men of any class without backbones, as well as lies, unwholesomeness, and all morbid rot—that was probably why his short, unsubtle, boyish sermons had a force, a driving-power, that made them tell, and why the men and boys he worked and played with loved him.

And Arnold, who was not there but ought to have been, had hated many things, and that was why he wasn't there.

Yes, they all hated something; they all rejected; all recognised without shirking the implied negations in what they loved. That was how and why they got things done, these vivid, living people. That was how and why anyone ever got anything done, in this perplexing, unfinished, rough-hewn world, with so much to do to it, and for it. An imperfect world, of course; if it were not, hate and rejections would not be necessary; a rough and ready, stupid muddle of a world, an incoherent, astonishing chaos of contradictions—but, after all, the world one has to live in and work in and fight in, using the weapons ready to hand. If one does not use them, if one rejects them as too blunt, too rough and ready, too inaccurate, for one's fine sense of truth, one is left weaponless, a non-combatant, a useless drifter from company to company, cast out of all in turn.... Better than that, surely, is any absurdity of party and creed, dogma and system. After all, when all is said in their despite, it is these that do the work.

Such were Eddy's broken and detached reflections in the course of this cheerful evening. The various pieces of counsel offered him by others were to the same effect. Blake Connolly, who, meeting him to-night for the first time, had taken a strong fancy to him, said confidentially and regretfully, "I hear the bride's a Tory; that's a pity, now. Don't let her have you corrupted. You've some fine Liberal sentiments; I used to read them in that queer paper of yours." (He ignored the fine Unionist sentiments he had also read in the queer paper.) "Don't let them run to waste. You should go on writing; you've a gift. Go on writing for the right things, sticking up for the right side. Be practical; get something done. As they used to say in the old days:

'Take a business tour through Munster,
Shoot a landlord; be of use.' "

"I will try," said Eddy, modestly. "Though I don't know that that is exactly in my line at present ... I'm not sure what I'm going to do, but I want to get some newspaper work."

"That's right. Write, the way you'll have public interest stirred up in the right things. I know you're of good dispositions from what Eily's told me of you. And why you want to go marrying a Tory passes me. But if you must you must, and I wouldn't for the world have you upset about it now at the eleventh hour."

Then came Traherne, wanting him to help in a boys' camp in September and undertake a night a week with clubs in the winter; and the elegant C.I.C.C.U. young man wanted him to promise his assistance to a Prayer-and-Total-Abstinence mission in November; and Nevill Bellairs wanted to introduce him to-morrow morning before the wedding to the editor of the *Conservative*, who had vacancies on his staff. To all these people who offered him fields for his energies he gave, not the ready acceptance he would have given of old, but indefinite answers.

"I can't tell you yet. I don't know. I'm going to think about it." For though he still knew that all of them were right, he knew also that he was going to make a choice, a series of choices, and he didn't know yet what in each case he would choose.

The party broke up at midnight. When the rest had dispersed, Eddy went home with Billy to Chelsea. He had given up the rooms he had shared with Arnold in Soho, and was staying with Billy till his marriage. They walked to Chelsea by way of the Embankment. By the time they got to Battersea Bridge (Billy lived at the river end of Beaufort Street) the beginnings of the dawn were paling the river. They stood for a little and watched it; watched London sprawling east and west in murmuring sleep, vast and golden-eyed.

"One must," speculated Eddy aloud, after a long silence, "be content, then, to shut one's eyes to all of it—to all of everything—except one little piece. One has got to be deaf and blind—a bigot, seeing only one thing at once. That, it seems, is the only way to get to work in this extraordinary world. One's got to turn one's back on nearly all truth. One leaves it, I suppose, to the philosophers and artists and poets. Truth is for them. Truth, Billy, is perhaps for you. But it's not for the common person like me. For us it is a choice between truth and life; they're not compatible. Well, one's got to live; that seems certain.... What do *you* think?"

"I'm not aware," said Billy, drowsily watching the grey dream-city, "of the incompatibility you mention."

"I didn't suppose you were," said Eddy. "Your business is to see and record. You can look at all life at once—all of it you can manage, that is. My job isn't to see or talk, but (I am told) to 'take a business tour through Munster, shoot a landlord, be of use.' ... Well, I suppose truth can look after itself without my help; that's one comfort. The synthesis is there all right, even if we all say it isn't.... After to-night I am going to talk, not of Truth but of *the* Truth; my own particular brand of it."

Billy looked sceptical. "And which is your own particular brand?"

"I'm not sure yet. But I'm going to find out before morning. I must know before to-morrow. Molly must have a bigot to marry."

"I take it your marriage is upsetting your mental balance," said Billy tranquilly, with the common sense of the poet. "You'd better go to bed."

Eddy laughed. "Upsetting my balance! Well, it reasonably might. What should, if not marriage? After all, it has its importance. Come in, Billy, and while you sleep I will decide on my future opinions. It will be much more exciting than choosing a new suit of clothes, because I'm going to wear them for always."

Billy murmured some poetry as they turned up Beaufort Street.

"The brute, untroubled by gifts of soul,
Sees life single and sees it whole.
Man, the better of brutes by wit,
Sees life double and sees it split."

"I don't see," he added, "that it can matter very much what opinions one has, if any, about party politics, for instance."

Eddy said, "No, you wouldn't see it, of course, because you're a poet. I'm not."

"You'd better become one," said Billy, "if it would solve your difficulties. It's very little trouble indeed really, you know. Anyone can be a poet; in fact, practically all Cambridge people are, except you; I can't imagine why you're not. It's really rather a refreshing change; only I should think it often leads people to mistake you for an Oxford man, which must be rather distressing for you. Now I'm going to bed. Hadn't you better, too?"

But Eddy had something to do before he went to bed. By the grey light that came through the open window of the sitting-room, he found a pack of cards, and sat down to decide his opinions. First he wrote a list of all the societies he belonged to; they filled a sheet of note-paper. Then he went through them, coupling each two which, he had discovered, struck the ordinary person as incompatible; then, if he had no preference for either of the two, he cut. He cut, for instance, between the League of Young Liberals and the Primrose League. The Young Liberals had it.

"Molly will be a little disappointed in me," he murmured, and crossed off the Primrose League from his list. "And I expect it would be generally thought that I ought to cross off the Tariff Reform League, too." He did so, then proceeded to weigh the Young Liberals against all the Socialist societies he belonged to (such as the Anti-sweating League, the National Service League, the Eugenics Society, and many others), for even he could see that these two ways of thought did not go well together. He might possibly have been a Socialist and a Primrose Leaguer, but he could not, as the world looks at such things, be a Socialist and a Liberal. He chose to be a Socialist, believing that that was the way, at the moment, to get most done.

"Very good," he commented, writing it down. "A bigoted Socialist. That will have the advantage that Traherne will let me help with the clubs. Now for the Church."

The Church question also he decided without recourse to chance. As he meant to continue to belong to the Church of England, he crossed off from the list the Free Thought League and the Theosophist Society. It remained that he should choose between the various Church societies he belonged to, such as the Church Progress Society (High and Modernist), the E. C. U. (High and not Modernist), the Liberal Churchmen's League (Broad), and the Evangelical Affiance (Low). Of these he selected that system of thought that seemed to him to go most suitably with the Socialism he was already pledged to; he would be a bigoted High Church Modernist, and hate Broad Churchmen, Evangelicals, Anglican Individualists, Ultramontane Romans, Atheists, and (particularly) German Liberal Protestants.

"Father will be disappointed in me, I'm afraid," he reflected.

Then he weighed the Church Defence Society against the Society for the Liberation of Religion from State Patronage and Control, found neither wanting, but concluded that as a Socialist he ought to support the former, so wrote himself down an enemy of Disestablishment, remarking, "Father will be better pleased this time." Then he dealt with the Sunday Society (for the opening of museums, etc., on that day) as incongruous with the Lord's Day Observance Society; the Sunday Society had it. Turning to the arts, he supposed regretfully that some people would think it inconsistent to belong both to the League for the Encouragement and Better Appreciation of Post Impressionism, and to that for the Maintenance of the Principles of Classical Art; or to the Society for Encouraging the Realistic School of Modern Verse, and to the Poetry Society (which does not do this.) Then it struck him that the Factory Increase League clashed with the Coal Smoke Abatement Society, that the Back to the Land League was perhaps incompatible with the Society for the Preservation of Objects of Historic Interest in the Countryside; that one should not subscribe both to the National Arts Collections Fund, and to the Maintenance of Cordial Trans-Atlantic Relations; to the Charity Organisation Society, and to the Salvation Army Shelters Fund.

Many other such discrepancies of thought and ideal he found in himself and corrected, either by choice or, more often (so equally good did both alternatives as a rule seem to him to be) by the hand of chance. It was not till after four o'clock on his wedding morning, when the midsummer-day sunrise was gilding the river and breaking into the room, that he stood up, cramped and stiff and weary, but a homogeneous and consistent whole, ready at last for bigotry to seal him for her own. He would yield himself unflinchingly to her hand; she should, in the course of the long years, stamp him utterly into shape. He looked ahead, as he leant out of the window and breathed in the clear morning air, and saw his future life outspreading. What a lot he would be able to accomplish, now that he was going to see one angle only of life and believe in it so exclusively that he would think it the whole. Already he felt the approaches of this desirable state. It would approach, he believed, rapidly, now that he was no longer to be distracted by divergent interests, torn by opposing claims on his sympathy. He saw himself a writer for the press (but he really must remember to write no more for the Conservative press, or the Liberal). He would hate Conservatism, detest Liberalism; he would believe that Socialists alone were actuated by their well-known sense of political equity and sound economics. In working, as he meant to do, in Datcherd's settlement, he would be as fanatically political as Datcherd himself had been. Molly might slightly regret this, because of the different tenets of Nevill and the rest of her family; but she was too sensible really to mind. He saw her and himself living their happy, and, he hoped, not useless life, in the little house they had taken in Elm Park Road, Chelsea (they had not succeeded in ousting the inhabitants of the Osiers). He would be writing for some paper, and working every evening in the Lea Bridge Settlement, and Molly would help him there with the girls' clubs; she was keen on that sort of thing, and did it well. They would have many friends; the Bellairs' relations and connections were numerous, and often military or naval; and there would be Nevill and his friends, so hard-working, so useful, so tidy, so well-bred; and their own friends, the friends they made, the friends they had had before.... It was at this point that the picture grew a little less vivid and clearly-outlined, and had to be painted in with great decision. Of course they came into the picture, Jane and Billy and the rest, and perhaps sometime, when she and Molly had both changed their minds about it, Eileen; of course they would all be there, coming in and out and mixing up amicably with the Bellairs contingent, and pleasing and being pleased by Nevill and his well-behaved friends, and liking to talk to Molly and she to them. Why not? Eileen had surely been wrong about that; his friendships weren't, couldn't be, part of the price he had to pay for his marriage, or even for his bigotry. With a determined hand he painted them into the picture, and produced a surprising, crowded jumble of visitors in the little house—artists, colonels, journalists, civil servants, poets, members of Parliament, settlement workers, actors, and clergymen.... He must remember, of course, that he disliked Conservatism, Atheism, and Individualism; but that, he thought, need be no barrier between him and the holders of these unfortunate views. And any surprisingness, any lack of realism, in the picture he had painted, he was firmly blind to.

So Molly and he would live and work together; work for the right things, war against the wrong. He had learnt how to set about working now; learnt to use the weapons ready to hand, the only weapons provided by the world for its battles. Using them, he would get accustomed to them; gradually he would become the Complete Bigot, as to the manner born, such a power has doing to react on the vision of those who do. Then and only then, when, for him, many-faced Truth had resolved itself into one, when he should see but little here below but see that little clear, when he could say from the heart, "I believe Tariff Reformers, Unionists, Liberals, Individualists, Roman Catholics, Protestants, Dissenters, Vegetarians, and all others with whom I disagree, to be absolutely in the wrong; I believe that I and those who think like me possess not merely truth but *the* truth"—then, and only then would he be able to set to work and get something done....

Who should say it was not worth the price?

Having completed the task he had set himself, Eddy was now free to indulge in reflections more suited to a wedding morning. These reflections were of the happy and absorbing nature customary in a person in his situation; they may, in fact, be so easily imagined that they need not here be set down. Having abandoned himself to them for half an hour, he went to bed, to rest before his laborious life. For let no one think he can become a bigot without much energy of mind and will. It is not a road one can slip into unawares, as it were, like the primrose paths of life—the novelist's, for example, the poet's, or the tramp's. It needs fibre; a man has to brace himself, set his teeth, shut his eyes, and plunge with a courageous blindness.

Five o'clock struck before Eddy went to bed. He hoped to leave it at seven, in order to start betimes upon so strenuous a career.

www.ingramcontent.com/pod-product-compliance
Lightning Source LLC
Chambersburg PA
CBHW072140270326
41931CB00010B/1819